WITHDRAWN

Stewart Bronfeld was a producer-writer for the NBC Television Network for more than sixteen years. In addition to producing, he has written many network television programs, as well as films released by Columbia Pictures and Universal Pictures. He is the author of *Writing for Film and Television* (Prentice-Hall, 1981), a Book-of-the-Month Quality Paperback selection, used as a text at many colleges and universities. He has produced hundreds of films, many of which have won awards, and has taught at several colleges and universities, including Yale University.

HOW TO PRODUCE A FILM

Stewart Bronfeld

A SPECTRUM BOOK
Prentice-Hall, Inc., Englewood Cliffs, New Jersey 07632

Library of Congress Cataloging in Publication Data

Bronfeld, Stewart.
How to produce a film.

"A Spectrum Book."
Includes index.

1. Moving-pictures—Production and direction—Handbooks, manuals, etc. I. Title.

PN1995.9.P7B65 1984 792'.0232 84-3334
ISBN 0-13-429432-7
ISBN 0-13-429424-6 (pbk.)

This book is available at a special discount when ordered in bulk quantities. Contact Prentice-Hall, Inc., General Publishing Division, Special Sales, Englewood Cliffs, N.J. 07632.

Editorial/production supervision by Peter Jordan
Cover design © 1984 by Jeannette Jacobs
Manufacturing buyer: Edward J. Ellis

A Spectrum Book. Printed in the United States of America.

2 3 4 5 6 7 8 9 10

ISBN 0-13-429432-7

ISBN 0-13-429424-6 {PBK.}

Prentice-Hall International, Inc., *London*
Prentice-Hall of Australia Pty. Limited, *Sydney*
Prentice-Hall Canada Inc., *Toronto*
Prentice-Hall of India Private Limited, *New Delhi*
Prentice-Hall of Japan, Inc., *Tokyo*
Prentice-Hall of Southeast Asia Pte. Ltd., *Singapore*
Whitehall Books Limited, *Wellington, New Zealand*
Editora Prentice-Hall do Brasil Ltda., *Rio de Janeiro*

With love to
Beverly Hanson Bronfeld,
without whose support and forbearance
this book would still be part of a tree in Oregon.

CONTENTS

HOW TO PRODUCE A FILM

PREFACE

The techniques of production are basically the same for any film, whether it is a two-hour movie, a twenty-minute corporate film, a student's three-minute film course assignment, or a ten-second television spot.

This book clearly shows how a film is produced from the original concept to the completed prints, in a series of decisions by the film's producer.

The reasons behind each decision, both creative and technical, are thoroughly explained at every step of the production process, so the prospective film producer not only will always know what to do, but will also understand *why*.

The Contents reveals that the book is as comprehensive as possible in scope. But what I feel is equally important is that each page realistically reflects the experience of today's working professional film producer.

S.B.

I am grateful to the following friends and professional colleagues, for valuable advice and assistance:

Vic Roby, National Broadcasting Company
Peter Page, Magno Sound Studios, New York
Richard Lavsky, Music House, Inc., New York
Jeffrey L. Burrows, Eastman Kodak Company
Eli L. Levitan
Lucien P. Fallot

HOW TO PRODUCE A FILM

1

THE BASIC TOOL

The act of transforming words on paper into reels of actual film depends most heavily on a piece of equipment not found in camera cases or cutting rooms or labs. It is portable, for it is installed deep in the skull: The basic tool of film production is the brain.

Producers usually know the strategy out of which their assignments come. They may even have sat in the panelled rooms where policy was made and contributed their thoughts to its development. But here we are concerned with the point at which a producer already has the assignment and sets about the job of producing a film.

The dictionary defines the verb *produce* as *to create; to bring forth.* The act of creating anything is a heady one, but to start with something as abstract as a scripted idea and bring forth something as tangible as a completed film is an accomplishment indeed.

To do it, the producer turns to the basic tool of film production, and using it, starts to think.

A TOOL CALLED MONEY: THE BUDGET

As the producer sits quietly thinking, there are many different factors guiding and directing his or her thoughts along the pathways of invention. But the most meaningful one is the budget. The budget, more than anything else, tells the experienced filmmaker what type of film will be produced, how much time it must take, and just how high creative fancies can soar when working on it.

When asked to produce a film, the first question one logically would ask is "What kind of film?" But the very next question should be "What is the budget?" The two questions should be considered a set, for they belong close together, and producers who let a lot of conversation get between the two questions are merely postponing the moment when they have a clear and realistic idea of exactly what they will have to do.

To illustrate, let us say that producer John Jones is assigned to make a three-minute promotional film for a new chewing gum product, to be shown to prospective distributors. "What kind of film do you have in mind?" John asks.

"It's for the big city markets," he is told. "The approach is, we're all getting crowded in by the concrete jungle. Life in large urban areas is too crowded, too busy, too noisy. There's not a lot you can do about it, without moving out, but you *can* do one thing—chew

Mountaindale Gum. It's got the flavor of the great unspoiled outdoors."

Even while our film producer listens, a number of probabilities come to his mind:

1. The "great unspoiled outdoors" will be represented somehow.
2. Life in the hectic, busy city will be demonstrated.
3. Some kind of special effect probably will be needed to show a couple of city dwellers propelled to the open country while they simultaneously remain in the city, as soon as they start to chew the gum.

These three general plans occur to him while he listens, but until he learns what the budget for the film is, he cannot be sure how they might be accomplished. On the one hand, if the budget is adequate:

1. He would take a film crew, equipment, whatever actors are needed, and possibly some staff members, to an appropriate "great outdoors" location for a few days.
2. He would shoot some scenes in his own or some other big city in such a way that the very *essence* of urban life is captured, rather than mere depiction of how crowded it is.
3. In devising a new visual means of showing two people enjoying the roomy vastness of a natural Eden while simultaneously being jostled by the crowds on a city street, he and some special effects experts would be free to ascend to heights of creativity bound only by the limits of their own imaginations.

On the other hand, if the budget is somewhat limited, then:

1. He would have to find his Eden not too far beyond the city limits, perhaps shooting very narrowly because a wider shot might reveal that they are actually in the suburbs.
2. He would have to film local shots which simply show how crowded and hectic big city life is, and try to plan them carefully so they come close to suggesting not only what crowding *is* but also what it *does* to a person, if possible.
3. The "simultaneous city/countryside" special effect, if any, would be limited to something like a familiar split screen.

If, however, the budget is downright *small,* it is an entirely different assignment, and a much more challenging one. It is a familiar fact of film production that a large budget permits creativity; a small budget *compels* it.

He would have to find things which somehow *symbolize* hectic city life and the calm outdoors with which he must contrast it. If he cannot discover these symbols he will have to create them, and then somehow succeed in convincing viewers that what they see on the screen is what the producer *says* they are seeing.

Unfortunately, some filmmakers are aware of the budget only as a restrictive force which places limits on their art. Others are not aware of the budget at all much of the time, until they find themselves trapped by unforeseen problems which can be solved only by shaking the budget and hoping that a few extra dollars will miraculously fall out. The successful producer, however, is always aware of the budget as a tool which, like any other tool, can impede the work at hand if used wrongly and aid it if used properly.

There is another lesson to be learned by the producer of a prospective film: to try to come up with brilliant flashes of inspiration *before* the wheels of production start turning. Take John Jones, our chewing gum promotional film producer, for example.

After becoming thoroughly familiar with his budget, he sits behind a cup of coffee in a creative reverie, his imagination roaming freely, seeking a clever new way to present on film the impact of a crowded city upon the people who live in it. He opens his mind to be receptive to a Great New Idea. Then it comes—a way of using scenes which he will shoot in a certain way to be later subjected to complex optical effects. It is original, clever, and will perfectly accomplish his objective.

It is also costly, for the required shooting will be extensive, and the optical effects to follow will entail specially made components. But an expensive idea that occurs at this stage can still be fitted intelligently into the budget, by examining existing plans in the light of this particular item's cost.

Accordingly, he looks at the tentatively drafted shooting schedule. Here, instead of taking along a production secretary from his office to the filming site in a distant state, he will hire a qualified local resident for a day or two. This will cost a comparatively modest hourly rate, and save the round-trip plane fare, motel and living expenses of a staff member. And here, he had planned to rent a station wagon for the camera crew and their equipment, plus a sedan to provide additional mobility. That would be convenient, but not essential; he cancels plans for the extra car.

Perhaps he feels these two savings will safely compensate for the extra money it will cost to execute his brilliant idea. If not, he can examine the budget further, to see if he can eliminate some other, more substantial outlay. For example, he might decide in advance that he will buy and use "canned" music for the film's background, thereby saving the expense of a composer, arranger and musicians, plus studio recording facilities.*

*The use of commercial music libraries is discussed in Chapter 9, *Music On Film.*

At this point, he can manipulate the budget to accommodate his changing ideas. But if an expensive idea comes to him later, while away on location for example, he has fewer options—the production secretary is already on the scene, sitting in the extra car which has already been rented; the composer may already be hard at work writing original music and will have to be paid, and a group of musicians may have been given firm commitments. And so, looking in the budget for items he can reduce or eliminate, he may find that the only way he can pay for *this* great idea is by sacrificing some *other* great idea.

This, incidentally, is no little sacrifice, for nothing is as hard to digest as a great idea that you have had to swallow. The agony can be so acute, in fact, that some film producers cannot bear to make the choice between two favorite production ideas when they really can afford only one of them—so they recklessly close their eyes and forge ahead with both. They know they are attempting an impossible balancing feat, but they tell themselves that somehow they can pull it off. Unfortunately, the only thing that may come off is the producer, eventually, from the payroll. In a filmmaker, many irksome little personality flaws may be tolerated—corruption, homicide, even treason; but the filmmaker who is known to indulge in the really *serious* vice of going over-budget has gone too far.

As with any other kind of budget, then, the film production budget is like a scale that must always be kept in balance. If you add something here, you must take something away there. It sounds simple, but often it is not, because one of the characteristics of film production is an element of unpredictability.

Most films are not really *made;* more realistically, they *evolve,* for even the most carefully planned film is subject to some change, which may happen at any stage of its production—or afterward.

There are two primary reasons for this.

First, the producer of a film often has full creative responsibility but not full creative control. Usually some other person or persons must give approval to the final film, which means they must be consulted about, or at least shown, each of its successive stages.

While this is most typical of a nontheatrical film, which a company's staff producer must submit to a corporate superior and an independent producer must submit to a client, it is by no means uncommon in the production of the conventional movie.

Among the many legends of Hollywood is that of the director as an absolute monarch, exercising total control. In reality, this was never widely prevalent in the actual workaday world of movie-making, being reserved for people such as Cecil B. De Mille and a few others who functioned simultaneously as both producer and director, as some do today. However, just as the phenomenon of absolute monarchy is fading in the capitals of the world, it is seen less and less in Hollywood.

This is a matter not of mores but of money. Movies are now so incredibly expensive to produce, and also to distribute and promote, that the concept of a filmmaker acting in solitary grandeur, answering to nobody until his or her film is in the can, is more myth than reality. The filmmakers creating the multimillion-dollar Hollywood epic and the low-budget *cinéma vérité* art film both must answer to the people controlling the budget, whose money entitles them to express opinions, suggestions or demands that can translate into changes in the film.

This matter of others changing the film you are making is, or can be, a somewhat sensitive area. It is to be expected that in considering any kind of project, people may have differing opinions on what is good or bad, effective or ineffective, necessary or unnecessary. The sensible person weighs the opinions of others and, upon logical reflection, may concede their merits. But when the project is a *creative* one, the issues are not so susceptible to agreement on what is "right" or "wrong." Creative judgments are acutely subjective; the creative person simply *feels* that something is right as often as he or she logically *thinks* that it is. Thus occasional disagreements about creative matters are inevitable.

When two creative people are involved, there may be a conflict between the inner vision of each; but when one of them is a relatively uncreative person it can be somewhat worse, because that person may disagree quite definitely but be unable to mitigate the problem of disagreement by offering useful creative suggestions.

In any event, the fact that filmmakers often must make changes because of the opinions of others can be viewed from either of two perspectives. By filmmakers whose egos are a predominant force in their work, it will be resented as interference. By filmmakers who, although quite healthy of ego, are aware of the broader goal of getting the job done successfully, it may be viewed more positively: being required to regularly consult with others can be a welcome relief from the lonely responsibility that marks professional creativity.

The second reason why the typical film is subject to possible change during the course of its production is simply because all plans, no matter how carefully made, can be affected by things that unexpectedly happen, or just as unexpectedly fail to happen. A factory, in which a sequence is to be shot for a business film, closes down indefinitely. An expert who is scheduled to lend on-camera authority to some dictum in an educational film is now unavailable. A museum which agreed to allow cameras to shoot a scene of a film amidst its masterpieces has had second thoughts and rescinds permission.

This, the evolutionary nature of a film's production, is clearly reflected in my files, as it would be in the files of any experienced producer. In each folder representing a film project, I see that the contents cited in the initial proposal are somewhat different from the contents of the script outline; the outline differs from the first draft of the script; and the script reveals changes, to one degree or another, in each subsequent draft. Even the "final" shooting scripts differ somewhat from what you would see in the actual films if you put them on a projector and screened them.

The unexpected sudden change may be manifested in a minor surprise, or by a potentially major problem—for which the remedy is usually money. Thus how well you use a budget, the second of the film producer's three primary tools, depends upon your use of the first: by starting each new production not by *doing* but by *thinking.* That way, you will also make maximum use of the most interesting tool of all—the tool of time.

A TOOL CALLED TIME

In film, there is no objective reality. There is only a controlled reality, created first by the scriptwriter and then manipulated by the filmmaker. In this controlled reality, familiar concepts such as *large, small, fast, slow* have no independent meaning, but are, instead, whatever the filmmaker establishes them to be.

A keyhole is small—but only when seen as it usually is seen by us. On film in a closeup it is large, and in an extreme closeup it is a vast chasm.

On film the perception of the same scene, with the same action and dialogue, can be changed from *fast* to *slow* and vice versa, solely by changing the dramatic context. For example, let us envision a scene in which a woman and a man are walking in a wooded glade. They are fellow house guests at a friend's weekend estate:

MAN

Nice scenery.

WOMAN

Yes, especially in this lovely fading light.

MAN

You're right. The sun is going down. I didn't notice.

WOMAN
Let's keep walking until it's completely dark.

MAN
All right.

A rather slow-moving scene.

Now let us change the context. A deranged strangler has killed three people in the area. The audience does not know who the killer is, except that he or she always strikes at night. Now, go back and again read the same scene, which still runs exactly the same length on film, with the same action and the same dialogue—but now is definitely not "slow."

Film producers often think of time as something palpable enough to be used—and in the using, possibly stretched, shortened, and even temporarily stopped. Such things are contradictions of natural laws in the real world, but not in film production, or in any area of activity involving changeable deadlines.

To illustrate, let us assume that because of an unexpected change, producer Jane Smith must complete a phase of her operation—the shooting of parts of her negative at the optical house—by tomorrow morning, which is twelve hours away. But the re-shooting would take thirty hours if done in the usual way, by a crew working at an optical printer. So she *buys* the extra eighteen hours she needs by assigning the task not to one optical house, but to several, working simultaneously on different scenes, which will accomplish the thirty-hour job in the twelve hours which actually exist.

This method of enlarging the supply of available time by simply buying it like bread, while effective, can be painfully expensive, especially during night hours when compound overtime rates may apply. Therefore, except for emergencies, filmmakers often use an alternate method of accomplishing this maneuver, which is just as effective and much more economical—*preplanning.*

In preplanning, the producer wields the tool of time in a way that is not only more practical but also more satisfying. Causing extra hours to materialize by using one's *dollars* is the act of a tradesman; working this same alchemy by using one's *brain* is the act of an artist.

Ideally, preplanning begins at the moment when, as we have seen, the producer with a new assignment sits down and quietly starts to think. We saw him trying to make intelligent use of his budget by relating it to a tentative production schedule he had

drafted. That schedule, no matter how sketchy it may be at first, helps to formulate general plans for a budget. And in most aspects of a film production budget, money and time, like water and ice, are actually two forms of the same thing.

The producer who explores various alternatives to his or her plans with a cinematographer or a sound engineer or an actor is acting wisely—*if* at the time the cinematographer is not on the set with the rest of the crew, ready to start shooting; and the sound engineer is not in the midst of a recording session; and the actor is not standing before the camera and about to deliver a line. "Talk is cheap" according to the old saying, but the old sayer should have added "only before production begins."

A prime element in preplanning is a producer's ability to *continually envision the completed film, in all its parts, as it will be in its final form.* The producer who does so is more likely to be spared the unwelcome discovery that a particular decision or idea, which seemed so clever and creative at the time, has caused inevitable problems at some later point in the production process.

Whether called producer or director or anything else, the person with the responsibility for making a film is often the only one to consider it in its entire context. At the start and all throughout production, others will be especially interested in various aspects—the general concept, how certain elements will be presented, individual parts involving their own contributions. But the producer, standing like a ringmaster in the center of it all, must always think of the film as a whole.

4 THE SCRIPT

"Create, artist! Do not talk!" said Goethe. Taking his advice, all the suggestions, proposals and possibilities of the planning stage are left behind, and now a specific description of the film is about to be committed to paper.

Whether the producer personally writes the script or assigns the writing to someone else, it is an important responsibility. More than any other production step, the script contains the seeds of the film's ultimate success or failure, since it largely determines how the finished film, in all its varying parts, will look and sound—and, most important, what it will *do*. For, ideally, every film, no matter what kind it may be or where it may be shown, has some purpose.

This purpose is, of course, quite clear to the producer of a film intended for marketing, education, promotion, or similar uses; but the creator of a theatrical film may not think of it as being required to "do" anything beyond entertaining its audience. If so, he or she would be wrong, and consequently the film could lack a vital element which makes the difference between a poor film and a good one, or between a good film and a great one. For the most artistic movie, just as the most sales-oriented business film, should reach out from the screen and have some measurable effect upon its viewers. Beyond merely holding their attention, it should somehow influence what they do or how they think or what they feel. Thus, the ultimate judgment of any film is not merely "Is it interesting?", but rather, "Does it have any impact?"

As we consider the many qualities that can make a script effective, it is important to emphasize one that is perhaps more essential than all the rest—*flexibility.* As the producer prepares to write or assign the outline, which is the precursor of the script, he or she must be sure that neither the outline nor the script ever become so fixed in their contents that any revision becomes a hardship—so that the film being blueprinted may, during production, be changed without major problems if necessary.

While any phase of a film's production is subject to change, the script is especially vulnerable. This is because, unlike other creative matrixes such as a painter's canvas or a composer's work score, a script is usually susceptible to the input of other people—a producer, director, employer, client, etc.—while it is being written.

On a nearby shelf is a pile of scripts, part of the flow of production material coming into my office at NBC over the years in relation to my work. I recently went to the pile and picked up a dozen of the scripts at random, a representative sampling of movies and television programs from the major studios such as Paramount, Columbia and 20th Century-Fox, as well as independent production companies such as Quinn Martin, MTM and Ross Hunter.

Since the scripts in the pile are production scripts—mimeographed copies distributed to cast, crew, and staff for use in the actual production—they are all, of course, final drafts, and most of them had probably been revised into at least third and often sixth and seventh drafts before arriving at the final draft. But the title pages reveal how "final" any final draft really is. Of the dozen I happened to pick up, five are marked FINAL DRAFT—but four others say REVISED FINAL DRAFT, and the other three all are marked SECOND REVISED FINAL DRAFT. A familiar Hollywood maxim sums it up best, in observing that "Scripts are not written; they're rewritten."

THEATRICAL AND NONTHEATRICAL SCRIPTS

There are two kinds of scripts, reflecting the fact that there are two basic kinds of films—those designed solely to entertain; and those with the more practical purpose of informing, instructing, selling, or otherwise making a point, either subtly or directly. The line between the two kinds of films exists, but it is anything but sharply drawn, for many of the most successful entertainment films certainly provide

audiences with something more substantial than mere amusing distraction; and many of the most effective instructional or sales films derive their very effectiveness from the fact that they are so entertaining.

There is no single accepted or "official" name for either type of film. In general professional use, one often hears the one type described as "theatrical" or "dramatic," and the other as either "nontheatrical," "industrial," "sponsored," or "audiovisual."

Strictly speaking, none of these are completely accurate. For example, many "nontheatrical" corporate films are seen as featurettes in small-town movie theatres; both kinds of films are actually "audiovisual" (as are slide-films); and schoolroom educational films are hardly "industrial."

However, while everyday use may be casually imprecise, our purposes here require that we be consistently specific. Therefore, throughout these pages let us use the terms *theatrical* and *nontheatrical* to designate the two kinds of films and their scripts.

It is seldom necessary to note any difference between the two categories in discussing film *production,* for in the camera, the cutting room, the sound studio and the lab, film is film, no matter what its intended audience may be. However, the scripts for the two types of films reflect two important differences.

First, nontheatrical scripts may be written in traditional dramatic fashion, across the whole page. But more often they are written in a format which divides each page in half: descriptions of visual elements on the left, and all sound, including speech, on the right. This is especially useful for films with narration, for words and picture of each scene are clearly aligned on the page as they will be seen and heard on the screen.

More important, the two types of films require two different kinds of writing. The special considerations of the theatrical film script are fully covered in *Writing for Film and Television,** an entire book devoted to that script genre. Therefore, let us here more fully explore what the film producer should strive for in the nontheatrical film script.

SCRIPTS AND SCRIPTWRITERS

A good script for any film should reflect its writer's ability to *think cinematically.* The producer should be aware that not every writer has the ability, or even the inclination, to write for the visual media.

*Stewart Bronfeld, *Writing for Film and Television* (Englewood Cliffs, N.J.: Prentice-Hall, Inc., 1981).

Some writers, in manifesting their creativity, think only in terms of words on paper. The visual writer, however, can also think creatively in cinematic terms, envisioning what he or she writes as it will be seen and heard on a screen.

Basically, prose writing *tells;* visual writing *shows.*

Just as every good writer is not necessarily a good scriptwriter, not every scriptwriter can write any kind of script with equal skill. For example, some theatrical scriptwriters may not be as adept in writing good narration as they are in writing good dialogue. And some nontheatrical scriptwriters who can convey uncomplicated ideas most effectively in a script may not have the rarer gift of making a complex subject understandable to the average viewer. On the other side of that coin are scriptwriters so experienced in making the complex seem clear that they oversimplify, out of habit, when it is not necessary or appropriate.

Finally, scriptwriters who have specialized in advertising and promotional films sometimes may not understand that poetic licenses are suspended when writing the script for an educational or training film, in which scrupulous accuracy is presumed.

THE OUTLINE

Sometimes, depending on the kind of film involved, a *storyboard* may be used before, in addition to, or even instead of, an outline. A storyboard is a series of blank squares on a sheet of paper, each square containing a hand-drawn sketch representing what will be seen in a scene, or possibly in an individual shot. Below each one is a blank space in which a brief description of the scene, or of the sound elements to accompany it, is written or typed.

A *planning board* is a movable storyboard, consisting of a series of individual index cards which can be freely inserted, removed, or switched around in their sequence. This may be simply done on a desk, or even on a floor, or it may more efficiently be done on a special board made or purchased for the purpose. When the concept and general organization of a film is finally reflected in the planning board to the producer's satisfaction, it may be photographed to become a storyboard, or a separate storyboard may be made.

Storyboards can be excellent tools for use in various stages of a film's development, but most especially when graphics are involved, because they can illustrate what the graphics will look like, *and* how they will work in the film, more realistically than a written outline.

In addition, because an outline flows from one sentence and paragraph to another, it sometimes can give a sense of continuity which may not in fact exist; a storyboard, however, shows scenes or shots as the individual entities they are, and their relationship to each other is more accurately reflected. Thus any choppiness in the sequence may be more apparent; and conversely, if a desired continuity is reflected in the storyboard, the producer can have more confidence that it will be achieved later on film.

Except in animation (which is discussed in Chapter 8), storyboards are often used at a point after the conception and preliminary development already have been worked out, to convey a sense of the proposed film to someone other than those involved in its creation. In the earlier stages, when ideas are still being considered and rejected, changed and combined, a planning board is more useful.

However, while planning boards and storyboards are valuable creative tools and do convey a cinematic image of the proposed film, they necessarily are limited to a somewhat terse and basic depiction. A more comprehensive and meaningful way of communicating what a film will be like, and why, is possible only in an outline.

A script outline can have two forms. An *outline* indicates the contents of a film; its more detailed form, the *treatment,* not only indicates the contents, but also gives some indication of how the contents will be conveyed to the viewer on the screen.

To illustrate this difference, the following is a brief portion of an outline for a film I wrote and produced for the NBC Television Network shortly before the Apollo 11 moon-landing mission.

> *4.* McGee [Frank McGee, the late NBC News correspondent], inside Mission Control in Houston, explains what will happen there on July 21st.

Later, in the treatment form of the outline, that portion, Scene #4, appeared as follows:

> *4.* McGee, inside Mission Control in Houston, leans against one of the telemetry consoles. Behind him, at other consoles, NASA workers are seen operating their equipment, talking on communications lines, etc. Turning, McGee points to a nearby man adjusting a headphone near his mouth, explaining that this man will be in constant moment-to-moment voice contact with all three astronauts. Then McGee reaches over and touches a switch. With a flick of this switch, he says, the man at this console can monitor the change in Neil Armstrong's heartbeat at the very moment he steps out of the LEM and puts the first footprint in human history on the surface of the moon.

This treatment portion's comparatively greater length is not what makes the difference, nor even that it contains more details. What makes it a treatment is that it goes beyond citing what Scene #4 is meant to accomplish, to also indicate *how* it will be accomplished on the screen.

A good scriptwriter avoids the temptation to crowd too much material in an outline. *The point is not how much information is packed into a film, but how much is left with the viewer.* A few key points, well made, will be remembered; too many key points become part of a blur of input, imperfectly recalled if not forgotten before *The End* fades from the screen.

In addition, the key points should be judiciously spaced so that one does not closely follow another, thus giving each one a chance to fully impress itself on the viewer's attention and memory.

WRITING NARRATION

Narration requires a somewhat special kind of writing skill. While all writers strive to make their writing as interesting as possible, the experienced nontheatrical scriptwriter is aware of the need for what might be termed controlled cleverness. Narration that is too cleverly written can be almost as undesirable as narration that is dull—because it is important that the audience not be distracted from *what* is said by *how* it is said.

If the prospective film is to contain existing footage, the scriptwriter should know this at the start, and be able to screen the footage, so that he or she does not waste time and creative effort in writing anything into the outline which could not really be matched by what will be on the screen.

In addition, before starting work on the actual script, the writer should note the exact length not only of various scenes but also of certain shots and parts of shots within each scene—whether existing footage or original shooting—so that, for example, the script will not contain fifteen seconds of narration for a shot which only lasts for nine seconds on the screen.

In writing and timing the narration copy to fit over specific shots and scenes, it would be well for the writer to remember two guidelines. First, narration or dialogue should always be timed while read fully aloud. If read silently against a stopwatch (a common error), the timing may be inaccurate by thirty percent or more, because delivering lines aloud requires that much more time to form consonants with lips and tongue and to manage intake of breath.

Second, those handy little words-per-minute tables, for use in estimating the length of written narration or dialogue, should generally be ignored. For years I have seen these tables in books and as parts of charts giving measurements of film footage, and I have always wondered at the folly of a formula based on a specific number of words per minute or words per second, for this blithely assumes that any two words, such as *it* and *indistinguishable,* take the same time to say aloud.

A more realistic guide for writing narration or dialogue to a specific time is to consider not words, but *syllables.* In general, narration or dialogue is spoken at the average rate of about three syllables per second. However, if a narrator has been selected before work begins on the script, the wise writer will obtain a recorded sample of the narrator's delivery so that a more accurate estimation may be made when writing to time.

A scriptwriter should be aware that spoken words on the screen vanish as soon as they are said. This places a special burden on the scriptwriter which the prose writer is spared. Not only must a scriptwriter's words be interesting and effective, but in addition they must be instantly comprehensible when heard from the screen.

An indispensable ingredient in the script of a well-paced film is lean writing. "Lean writing" does not necessarily mean writing that lacks depth, nor even length. It simply means that, like lean meat, there is no waste material that could be cut out and discarded. In a script, every line, every word that is not absolutely necessary should be eliminated. The inevitable result of this ruthless trimming is that the lines which remain, stripped of their dross, now sparkle with effectiveness.

One of the key components in the success of any film is viewer involvement, which can make the important difference between whether the viewer passively watches the film or actively experiences it.

This may be accomplished by establishing a sense of *identification* in the viewer. In theatrical scripts, for example, the identification is either with the characters in the story, because they reflect some universal human traits, or with the basic conflicts generating the drama, which are familiar in the lives of us all. Nontheatrical scripts can achieve viewer identification by using the language—professional or trade terms, regionalisms, ethnic references, etc.—of the film's intended audience as much as possible.

I know of no better overall advice about narration than what Jonathan Swift wrote about the art of conversation:

> *Give . . . always of the prime,*
> *And but little at a time.*

It usually will be found that a film needing less narration has been better planned, shot, and edited than one requiring an almost continuous voice over every scene, to "say" what the film is supposed to "show."

A film I produced for NBC shortly before a national election, about how such events were reported in colonial times in comparison with the election coverage of NBC News today, used a total of eleven seconds of narration, and received an International Broadcasting Award from the Hollywood Radio and Television Society that year.

One of my colleagues produced a documentary for NBC in Washington which contained only fifteen seconds of narration, and won an Emmy Award.

Narration is important, but human visual memory is stronger than auditory memory, and therefore an important goal of any film is to be visually articulate.

PREPARATION FOR FILMING

shown at the smallest neighborhood theatre and on television. However, the cost involved in shooting and processing a film in 70mm is so much greater than that of 16mm or 35mm that there is no reason to even consider 70mm production unless the film is scheduled for a substantial number of showings in wide-screen sites.

Therefore, for most professional film production the decision is really between 16mm and 35mm, or in some cases possibly combining the two.

Actually, the choice today is not so much a question of deciding between 16mm and 35mm, but rather whether there are any compelling reasons for *not* using 16mm, which is less expensive to work in, and offers much more mobility in shooting because of the smaller camera involved.

At one time, 35mm was the gauge that clearly marked the professional, with 16mm used only by advanced amateurs and quasi-professionals such as makers of films for their own schools or clubs. But today, the picture and sound quality, editing techniques, optical effects, processing, and duplicating potential once reserved only for 35mm film are now largely available to the filmmaker working in 16mm as well. It is not surprising, then, that *the bulk of all professional nontheatrical film production today is done in 16mm.*

Three kinds of films are produced primarily in 35mm: feature-length movies, both theatrical and made-for-TV; most one-hour dramatic series on television; and most national television commercials, including movie trailers and network promos. There are two principal reasons for this, relating to picture and sound.

The producers of movies, network television programs, and TV commercials require, and can afford, the utmost in picture and sound quality. A frame of 35mm film is four hundred percent greater in area than a 16mm frame. Therefore, during shooting it benefits photographically from interaction with that much more light. Then, during projection, being four times the size of 16mm to begin with, 35mm film can project an enlarged image onto a screen with far less degradation, if any.

In addition, because a 35mm sound track is greater in area and also moves faster than a 16mm track, there is a potential for much more fidelity and range in 35mm sound.

For these reasons, 35mm provides better picture and sound quality than 16mm. The question is, how *much* higher quality, and is it significant enough in a particular film to warrant the extra cost of 35mm production?

Quality, of course, is a relative concept. To the producer of a typical nontheatrical film, never meant for showing on a huge screen or on television, the answer might be that the extra picture and sound quality are not worth the greater expense. This is because, given the excellent results possible from the wide range of 16mm film types now available, it is not really a question of *fair versus good,* but rather, *good versus even better.*

However, the potential higher quality which 35mm may offer is not the only consideration. Movies, television series and TV commercials typically contain sophisticated optical effects. Most of these are accomplished technically by special cameras shooting series of multiple exposures (described more fully in Chapter 8). In such a process an all-important requirement is precise *registration,* which is the exact alignment of moving frames of film in a camera and on the pegs of an optical bench or animation stand, so that the multiple exposures will be positioned accurately. Since 35mm film has four perforations, or sprocket holes, on each side of every frame—compared to the one or two sprocket holes per frame of 16mm film—it can be engaged and held in place by the camera sprockets or the pegs much more surely and accurately, ensuring truer registration.

Therefore, if a producer contemplates a film—no matter what its purpose or potential audience—which will contain a substantial amount of important special effects, the ideal choice would be 35mm cameras and film.

If this film were primarily to be used on 16mm projectors, the producer could still shoot and process it in 35mm form, and then have a 16mm negative made of the completed film for use in printing 16mm *release prints,* the term applied to final prints ready for distribution.

However, if there were only a few important special effects, the producer could decide to make the film as a whole in 16mm, but to shoot the special effects material in 35mm and later reduce this segment to 16mm for integration into the rest of the film.

Finally, if the special effects were not particularly complex, they could be shot and processed in 16mm along with everything else.

The mixture of 16mm and 35mm material within a single production is not uncommon, as 16mm film can be enlarged—the term more often is "blown up"—to 35mm as easily as 35mm can be reduced to 16mm. But while neither procedure presents any problem technically, the producer must consider the extra cost of blow-up or reduction, as well as the loss of some picture quality when blowing up 16mm film to 35mm size.

This loss of quality results from the fact that the grain of the

16mm film is enlarged along with the picture content. The grain, of course, was always there, as it is in any film; but, in a comparatively smaller and more compact picture frame, it was less noticeable. Now, magnified significantly, that graininess is much more noticeable. (Conversely, since the grain in 35mm film is made smaller along with the picture content when reducing it to 16mm size, there is something of a gain in overall picture quality because of the reduction.)

This is another reason why films made to be shown in movie theatres are generally produced in 35mm. So many theatres only have 35mm projectors that a movie produced in 16mm would have to be blown up to 35mm size for mass printing, which could degrade its original picture quality to some degree.

Further, even if the 16mm print were shown in a conventionally-sized movie house which does have a 16mm projector, the enlargement involved in the picture's travel—or *throw*—onto the theatre-sized screen could work the same grainy mischief as enlargement in a lab.

Just how noticeable the loss in picture quality will be in enlarging 16mm to 35mm depends upon the graininess of the particular piece of 16mm film being used. Another consideration is the placement of the blown-up scene; if adjacent scenes are comparatively darker and busier, the heightened graininess of a blown-up segment will be that much less apparent.

The great advantage 16mm offers, which can sometimes transcend all other considerations, is its great mobility. Unlike its bulkier and heavier 35mm counterpart, a 16mm camera can easily be hand-held to shoot almost anywhere.

NEGATIVE VERSUS REVERSAL

Anybody who has ever used a still camera is somewhat familiar with the basic differences between negative and reversal film, although they may not use those terms.

Every snapshot-taker is aware that one kind of film, when put in for processing, will return prints and a negative, and the other gives you transparencies mounted as slides. Since no negative comes back with the slides, it is obvious that the film that was in the camera has somehow been made directly into the slides with no intervening photographic step. This one-step process, and the film it uses, is called *reversal*.

Film is film, whether the frames are printed on paper, mounted

individually as slides, or continuously attached and called motion picture footage. Therefore, in essence, the basic considerations of the Sunday afternoon photographer and that of the film producer are quite similar when it comes to choosing between negative and reversal film (except, of course, that the results of the film producer's decision are considerably more complex than an envelope of family pictures).

Until a few years ago, producing a film in 16mm always meant using reversal film, since negative film was available only in 35mm size. Then, in the 1950's, Eastman Kodak introduced negative film in the 16mm size as well, and the use of negative film in 16mm production has grown significantly among nontheatrical filmmakers, most especially in recent years.

However, while reversal and negative film are now both regularly used in 16mm, *the same is not true in 35mm filmmaking, which almost exclusively uses negative film.* In fact, there is no 35mm reversal film generally available.* Therefore, our discussion of the choice between negative and reversal relates only to 16mm film production.

After shooting with negative film, the exposed film is put into the lab for development into a negative, which is then used in making a separate positive print. But after shooting with reversal film, the exposed film is put into the lab where it *becomes* a positive print.

But remember: the reason a reversal print can come back from the lab so quickly, and at an initial saving in processing costs, is because there is no negative involved. If you require relatively few prints of your film, then you may have no real need for a negative and the reversal process could be the best choice. However, if you require multiple release prints in substantial quantities, you would find this method less desirable than if you had shot and processed negative film. It would depend on how many prints you needed, and also how quickly you needed them, as we shall see.

To obtain multiple prints when using reversal film, you do just what home photographers do when they want prints made from their slides: you send your reversal film back to the lab to be used in making special negatives, called *internegatives.* From these, a quantity of duplicate prints may be made. (If less than three prints are required, they may be printed directly from the original film

*Some does exist, but only for extremely specialized applications; for example, some *35mm Eastman Ektachrome Video News Film* is made primarily for those who need one film they can use either for still photos or motion pictures.

out of the camera onto special reversal printing stock, without the use of internegatives.)

However, you might be aware that the multiple prints you obtain from internegatives with reversal film are not quite equal in quality to prints you could obtain from negative film. For the snapshot-taker and the film producer the reason is the same: *the more intermediate steps there are between a print and the original film exposed in the camera, the less can be expected in overall picture quality.*

This potential loss in picture quality can manifest itself in overall graininess, lack of sharpness, and fading of original color tones. How great the loss actually will be depends in each case on the type and quality of the original film, and on how many steps, such as duplication or repeated reprinting of a negative, have intervened. The loss may very well be negligible, and thus not readily noticeable, although in extreme cases the graininess or the overall "washed out" look can be woefully obvious.

Extreme cases aside, however, despite its original introduction as a film to be put on a projector rather than to be reproduced in any quantity, today's color reversal film can be duplicated to provide reasonable numbers of release prints of very good quality (although not as good as prints from negative film). In addition, reversal film can satisfy the special requirements of certain filmmakers.

For example, because of the subject or the circumstances of the filming sessions for some films, a lot of footage is shot but only a fraction of it is used. In such a case, if the cameras were loaded with negative film, the filmmaker would have to pay for developing the negative and making a print of all of it, just to be able to screen what was shot.

Here, using reversal film would cut the costs significantly, because the large amount of footage would be available for screening and evaluation after one processing step,* and only the selected shots and scenes need be sent to the lab for internegatives. Many documentary films are produced with 16mm reversal film for just this reason.

Then, the fact that reversal can be used to achieve a more quickly produced film has been a problem solver for many filmmakers facing a harrowing schedule. I recall, more vividly than I prefer, some occasions at NBC when the reversal process made the difference between triumph and disaster as my deadline moved from the calendar to the wall clock.

*The screening would probably be on a viewer (described in chapter 8), which is more protective of film than a projector.

Another special requirement might be the need to shoot with mobility in color using very fast film under artificial light, such as at a nighttime football game. There is fast negative film available, but the fastest reversal film, although comparatively grainier, is even faster.

Thus, reversal film is especially useful in certain kinds of filmmaking, such as the production of local television commercials and promos, which are often printed only in small quantities; documentaries and experimental films, which usually shoot more footage than will be used; films that are topical, or that are assigned at the last minute, and therefore must be completed quickly; or any of a number of other kinds of production for which reversal film is uniquely suited, including those nontheatrical films which do not require a lot of prints.

On the other hand, negative film represents production without compromise.

Since it does not have to perform technical tricks in the processing lab, such as reversal's fast metamorphosis from a negative into a positive print, the chemical emulsion on negative film can be completely devoted to attaining better overall picture quality.

But it is in the duplication of prints that negative film even more clearly excels over reversal film. With negative film, even the thousandth release print, made from perhaps the fourth or fifth duplicate negative, will still have originated from a "grandfather negative" that was a better negative to start with, and the prints will show it.

COLOR VERSUS BLACK-AND-WHITE

Democritus, the Greek philosopher who espoused the atomic theory of matter some 1,500 years ago, wrote: "By convention there is color . . . but in reality there are atoms and space."

Though it may really be only atoms and space, audiences have come to expect color in every contemporary film they see, in theatres, board rooms, halls, and everywhere else that films are shown. Consequently, as with the decision between film gauges, the question is not so much a choice between color and black-and-white but rather whether there are any reasons *not* to film in color.

Three possible reasons for producing a film today in black-and-white might be considerations of cost, lighting conditions, or subject matter.

Color film costs more than black-and-white film. In addition, the cost of processing it is about double that for black-and-white. Film processing can be a significant factor in a budget, often not confined to a one-time expense for final prints. As we shall see, footage may be put into the lab for a number of film processing needs which can arise during a film's production.

This means that if a budget is unusually tight, the difference between processing costs for color and black-and-white could be a decisive factor. It is, after all, better to spend the limited dollars of a small budget on the shooting or editing or graphics which will make the film what you want it to be, rather than ending up with an abridged and deflated version of what you envisioned—but in glorious color.

Sometimes the choice of black-and-white film is dictated by the need to shoot under low lighting conditions. A film's need for light is greatly intensified when color is involved, for in photography, as in human vision, there *is* no perception of color without adequate light, as will be noted in a darkened room or on a dimly lit street at night. This is also evident in scenes in movies or television programs that take place in darkened locales, for even though there may have been color film in the camera when the scenes were shot, we see them primarily in black-and-white.

Therefore, in the case of a film whose every scene will be in a dark setting, a producer may very well decide to shoot it all in black-and-white, since there would be little, if any, return on the extra cost of color film and its processing.

However, a producer would have no choice but black-and-white film when shooting in *extremes* of low lighting, such as in a dark place where no supplementary lighting is possible. This is because, while today's color films are faster than ever before, they still are not as fast as the fastest black-and-white film. In low light, it may sometimes be a case of filming in black-and-white or not filming at all.

Finally, we come to the most interesting of all the possible reasons not to film in color.

Sometimes, when there is no problem of budget nor of lighting, a filmmaker may feel that the subject matter itself somehow warrants being filmed in black-and-white. I say "somehow" because here we are dealing with judgments not based on specifics such as technical standards. Decisions about subject matter are, as the word implies, necessarily subjective; personal perceptions and feelings are the decisive factors.

The ultimate goal of a filmmaker is to use the screen to present not merely *realism,* but *reality.* And, as experienced filmmakers know, many viewers have a tendency to equate reality with black-and-white. Color is beautiful but black-and-white is believable.

While I have only guesses and opinions about why audiences readily equate black-and-white with reality, I am much more certain of why they should not. Consider what a fascinating example it is of the wonderful perversity of human nature, that although we clearly live in a world of color, and color *should* therefore represent reality, nevertheless it is the absence of color which looks more real to many of us when seen on a screen.

Suppose you are contemplating a film, or perhaps part of a film, in which you hope to capture on the screen the essence of life in a squalid tenement—not just how it looks, but how it *is* to be trapped in a world of poverty amid grime and desolation. Picture, on the theatre screen in your mind, some shots of the wretched apartment, the tenement, the bleak neighborhood. Which would be more suitable, more effective in conveying not only the sights but also the feelings of the people involved—black-and-white or color?

John Ford, the great motion picture director, had the financial resources of 20th Century-Fox behind him when he directed *The Grapes of Wrath.* He decided to film it in black-and-white, and won an Academy Award for it.

Sir Laurence Olivier has had many triumphs, including his film of Shakespeare's *Henry V,* which he produced in color. Yet, when he directed and starred in *Hamlet,* he felt that this character, this story, would be more real to audiences in black-and-white. Apparently he was right, for the picture won Academy Awards for best picture and best actor.

There are many other examples, not only among Hollywood movies, but among business, educational, and other nontheatrical films as well. What their producers knew is that black-and-white is not always a compromise or a concession, but can, on the right occasion, be a decisive factor in successfully putting on the screen what the filmmaker is trying to convey.

STUDIO VERSUS LOCATION FILMING

If the script calls for a room deep within the secluded recesses of the Kremlin, the decision to shoot it on a studio set is obvious.

Conversely, if the script requires a narrator to speak from the Vehicle Assembly Building at Cape Kennedy, which has been called the largest room on earth, or while standing at a giant blast furnace in full operation inside a Pittsburgh steel mill, filming on location is clearly indicated.

Much of the time, however, the setting is in that middle ground of possibility requiring a filmmaker to come to a real decision about whether to shoot on location or in a studio.

There are good reasons for deciding either way.

Stage audiences, unlike film viewers, traditionally meet the producer more than halfway in accepting where the action is supposed to be happening. A makeshift bench, a few papier-mâché rocks, a picture of a bridge in the background, and the audience is quite willing to accept that they see "A hill in Golden Gate Park," as the printed program tells them.

The producer of a film, however, must give the audience a park and bridge that look real, not merely realistic. A location background can provide this expected authenticity to a scene far better than even the best studio set.

On the other hand, the possibility to control every component element, which gives the film production process its great creative potential, is fully realized in the film studio. The sound, the lighting, the weather, the movement of everyone and everything within camera range—all these and more are under the tight control of the filmmaker in a studio, built and equipped especially for the purpose.

Location shooting has been made vastly more convenient by the increased awareness of almost every state, and many major cities, of the economic value of film production. For example, most states and larger cities have a special office to assist filmmakers in finding suitable filming sites, by providing location scouts and special liaison arrangements with local authorities. Many states even offer special inducements to filmmakers, ranging from special tax abatements to free use of state-owned helicopters.

Some location shooting may be relatively inexpensive, such as filming the president of a corporation in his or her own office instead of renting a studio. In other types of location filming the possible additional expenses may be substantial: the cost of transporting people and equipment to and from the film site; possible construction of something that should be there but is not; rental of needed equipment, such as generators, special lights and sound units, etc.

There are also possible extra costs in time, which can affect a tight production schedule. For example, uncooperative weather can extend a two-day filming session to a week or more. In addition, filming must sometimes end before the day's planned footage has been shot, because the scene requires full daylight.

Finally, the very fact that the location *is* real invites potential intrusion of the regular activity that goes on in the outside world. And, with no studio door to lock, a location site abounds with cables and assorted gear for unexpected outsiders to trip on.

Still, an actual location setting can contribute a wealth of unmistakably authentic sights and sounds, investing a scene with an atmosphere impossible to duplicate in any studio—the ambience of real life.

THE TECHNIQUE OF SHOOTING FILM

The film producer's art is one of creative assembly, using a number of different elements. In their place, all make an equally significant contribution—but the shooting of film, like the Caesars of ancient Rome, is "first among equals."

It is with the audience in mind that a professional decides not only what to shoot on film, but also exactly how to shoot it. For the angle, the distance, the perspective of every shot, derive their importance from one basic fact—the camera is the eye of the audience.

OBJECTIVE AND SUBJECTIVE FILMING

By the way he or she uses the camera, a filmmaker can select the role the audience will assume in viewing a scene, or sometimes an entire film.

Objective filming, the more or less standard method, provides a view of the scene from the perspective of an observer who can see everyone and everything of interest. Thus the role of the audience is that of *spectator.*

Subjective filming shows the scene as viewed by a *participant.*

Most angles are either from the point of view of the people performing the action,* or from over their shoulders. This brings the audience *into* the film, instead of merely sitting and watching it.

While subjective filming may be useful in any kind of film, it is of particular value in educational, training, and general informational films. However, many scenes in such films are more effectively shot from an objective angle instead, which can provide a meaningful perspective by showing the relationship between various elements in a scene.

Many theatrical films contain individual scenes that have been shot subjectively. In addition, subjective shooting can help to solve the problem of movie adaptations of books written in the first person, in which that "first person feel" would otherwise defy transfer from the printed page onto the screen, despite voice-over narration by the story's protagonist.

However, subjective shooting in a theatrical film is at its most effective as a means of achieving identification on the part of an audience with people in the story—one of the key requisites for successful screen drama. Shooting subjectively accomplishes this sense of identification in two ways, one less apparent than the other.

First, repeated use of point-of-view angles obviously will link the viewer's orientation to that of the person whose perspective is so often represented by the camera.

But in addition, the frequent use of "as seen by" angles necessarily means that the main character, whose viewpoint is represented by the camera, is thereby not seen as often, adding to the audience's feeling that the story is happening from *their* viewpoint. When that happens, they care—which is often the prime difference between a film that merely interests an audience and one that has an impact on them.

MOTION PICTURE LIGHTING

Before there can be any kind of photography, whether snapshots or motion pictures, there must be light. But beyond merely providing essential illumination, lighting can be an important creative tool in filmmaking.

The atmosphere of a dramatic scene can be created by the artful placement of shadows, or the meaning of a look in someone's

*Point of view (POV) angles are discussed later in this chapter, in *Camera Shots.*

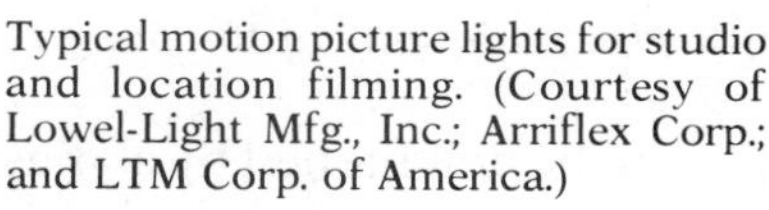

Typical motion picture lights for studio and location filming. (Courtesy of Lowel-Light Mfg., Inc.; Arriflex Corp.; and LTM Corp. of America.)

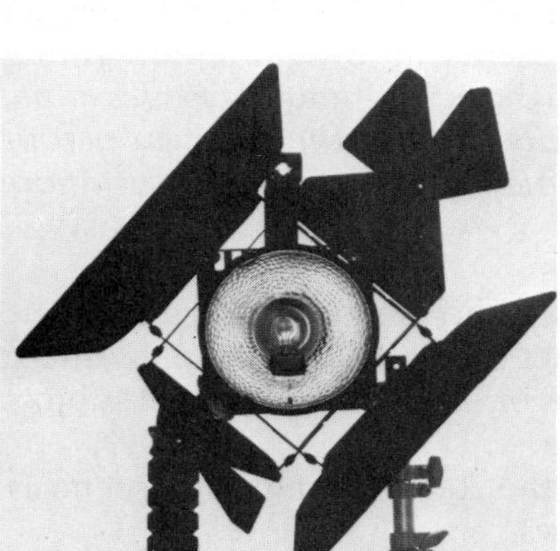

eyes can be heightened by planes of light on the face. In an industrial film, the gleam of bright lighting, sparkling here and there, transforms an ordinary machine room into the scene of exciting activity, and the somewhat stern-looking features of an interviewed executive are softened by the play of warm lighting around the eyes.

The lighting techniques for motion pictures are somewhat different from those for still pictures. The film is basically the same, but the camera and its subjects are not; in cinematography, they can *move,* and the lighting patterns often must accommodate this movement, both on the set and on location.

Lighting the Film Set Each scene of a film, and sometimes an individual shot within a scene, presents its own unique lighting requirement. There is, however, a basic technique. *Professional lighting of a motion picture set usually involves the interplay of four types of lighting, any of which may come from one or more individual lights.*

The Key Light. As the name implies, the key light represents the primary illumination for a scene, whether there is a principal camera subject, such as one or more persons or objects, or a general subject area.

The amount or intensity of the key lighting in a scene is generally determined by four factors:

1. The light that is appropriate and natural for that place at that time of day or night.
2. The physical dimensions of the set being lit.
3. Creative considerations, such as the desired atmosphere or mood for the scene.
4. The length of time that people in the scene will be subjected to the lights.

The overall result of the key lighting is described as either *high key* in the case of more brightly lit scenes, or *low key* for generally darker scenes (which is the origin of the familiar expression "low-keyed" for someone or something subdued or restrained.)

Sometimes entire films are lit one way or the other. For example, overall lighting for a horror movie is usually low key, and most comedies are almost entirely high key. (The glossy-bright lighting on television game shows, meant to enhance the frantic excitement, can only be called *hyper key.*)

Always the first to be set up, the key light, or group of lights, faces the subject at about a 45° angle (except for closeups which may call for direct head-on lighting) and is positioned high enough so that the angle of the light does not invite squinting on the part of people in the scene.

The Fill Light. Coming from the other side of a stationary camera, or from a light mounted directly on a moving camera, is *fill light,* designed to fill in, with its own softer light, the areas where shadows caused by the key light are obscuring some outlines or details.

The fill lighting is diffused by light-filtering material at the lens of each light, resulting in illumination that may be powerful but is not "bright." (The strong yet diffused fill light is the traditional favorite of aging movie stars.)

The Separating Light. Since the subject area may be somewhat bathed in light, it is often necessary to impart depth to the scene by separating the subject from the background.

This is usually accomplished by *backlight,* which lights the subject from behind, to make the subject emerge more clearly. Being opposite the camera, the backlight is high enough to be out of its range, avoiding possible lens flare.

For additional separation, another light, called a *kicker* because its rays are sharply reflective, is often trained on the subject from an angle opposite the key light.

Background Light. The use of lighting upon the background is more optional than the other three types of lighting.

When the background is part of the focus of interest on a large set, it may be specifically lit by high-hanging side lights; on a smaller set, it may be lit by hidden lights positioned behind a person or a piece of furniture.

Often, however, a creative effect such as low key lighting, or a practical need such as more clearly separating the subject from the surrounding area, may best be served by not lighting the background at all.

In other situations, the light reaching the background from the key and fill lighting, called *spill light,* is often deemed sufficient.

While the creative lighting of a set entails the blending of various lights of differing intensity, clarity, and broadness of beam, the mixing of lights with substantially different color quality is generally avoided.

The human eye readily adjusts to such differences, but the film in the camera does not. Consequently, what appears on the set as a barely noticeable variation in color quality between two lights may show up on the screen as a clearly seen, yet unexplained, difference in the color of adjacent parts of the same thing.

Shooting in Natural Light When filming outdoors one may not be able to completely control the light, but one *can* control its effects.

For example, unwanted shadows under chins and eyes, or too much overall contrast in a scene, are often encountered when shooting beneath a midday sun, but can be substantially reduced by filtering the overhead light through the meshlike material of a simple device made for the purpose, called a *scrim,* or by the use of fill-in artificial lighting.

In addition to the use of equipment to diffuse, block, or reflect sunlight or skylight, location filming often requires the cinematographer to shoot at special angles in dealing with the vagaries of the light source.

One of the prime considerations in shooting part or all of a film outdoors is balancing the light properly, so that shots which are made on separate days, but which will appear as part of the same scene, are identically lit.

Good motion picture lighting, above all, should look natural, because it is accepted by audiences as the light coming from the principal light source they see in the scene (a lamp, a window, etc.).

Thus, unlike stage lighting, motion picture lighting should never evoke admiring comment from the audience—for if they can *notice* it, the illusion has failed.

SHOOTING RATIOS

The *shooting ratio* describes the relationship between the amount of footage that is shot and the amount of that footage actually appearing in the completed film. For example, if 100 feet of film are shot to obtain a scene which ultimately will run 10 feet on the screen, the shooting ratio is 10-to-1.

While a shooting ratio can seldom be planned with total precision, a fairly realistic estimate is necessary in preparing a film budget because the shooting ratio affects three separate costs—the *raw stock,* which is the new, unexposed film; the actual filming time, since obviously the crew can shoot only as long as there is film for them to shoot with; and the processing of the film after it has been shot.

Shooting ratios depend on a number of different factors which vary with each film: the subject matter to be shot, the circumstances of the filming, even the style of the director.

Thus, while a truly "average" shooting ratio is impossible to cite, ratios ranging from 5-to-1 to 10-to-1 would not be considered unusual for shooting that is done from a script. However, in shooting documentaries and other films which may shoot the footage first and script a narration afterward, the shooting ratio could reach 50-to-1 or even higher, due to the lack of a specific list of scenes to shoot, which a prewritten script would provide.

There is a method of shooting called "editing in the camera," whereby all the shots are made in the order in which they will appear on the screen, thus using a shooting ratio of 1-to-1. This method is usually confined to amateur projects or professional films of an experimental nature, for besides the lack of creative control caused by the absence of any true editing, the 1-to-1 filmmaker may have to include imperfect takes and technically marred footage as part of the finished film.

SHOTS, SCENES, AND SEQUENCES

Any discussion of filming necessarily involves use of the words *shot, scene,* and *sequence,* whose meanings and relationship to each other are not always clearly understood.

A *shot* is the basic unit of film. Technically, it is any single, *continuous* portion of film exposed in the camera. Thus if a camera operator, while shooting some action, stops the camera for the merest moment and then without changing position or angle instantly starts it again, the result is two individual shots, even though the action would appear almost continuous if later seen on the screen. It is the "almost" here that makes the difference between one shot or two.

A *scene* generally consists of a number of different shots. It is the selection and placement of the shots that largely determines the nature and quality of the scene.

It is possible that a complete scene might actually consist of one continuous length of film. In such a case, while it would be referred to as a scene, in a strictly *technical* sense it is at the same time a shot. However, while not rare, single-shot scenes are the exception rather than the rule. More frequently, a number of different shots are the building blocks of any scene, especially in a dramatic film.

A *sequence* consists of a number of consecutive scenes which share some common theme, such as a chase sequence, a homecoming sequence, or a battle sequence. In nontheatrical films, the common theme is often one of subject matter rather than plot: a mountain-climbing sequence, a factory sequence, a desert sequence, etc.

A sequence should not be confused with a *montage,* in which a series of shots or scenes are presented at an unnatural pace, or appear simultaneously on a multi-split screen, to make a special point.

THE DRAMATIC FOCUS

Let us visualize the start of a scene being shot. The setting is the living room of a private home. A mother, sitting on a couch, is talking to her teenage daughter who is standing in the doorway. The father of the girl is in a nearby armchair, reading a newspaper. He is not actively taking part in the conversation between his wife and daughter, but he easily can listen to it:

MOTHER

You must have come home quite late
last night, dear. You said you'd
be home before eleven, but we went
to bed after two, and you weren't
in yet.

DAUGHTER

Well, I didn't think I'd stay too
long at the party. But then I met
Bobby Thompson there, and after it
was over we went for a hamburger
and a drive.

There are many ways to film this simple exchange of dialogue, but until we know more about the story, only one or two camera angles come to mind. We might frame a shot of the mother and daughter, since the father apparently is not involved in the dialogue. Or we might film the mother in a close shot, then the daughter in a close shot, and let the film editor later cut back and forth as they speak.

At this point, all we might aim for is a well-composed picture—because we do not know the *dramatic focus* of the dialogue.

To an objective observer, the maximum dramatic impact of an exchange of words is, depending on the context, focussed at one of three points: *(a)* the person speaking; *(b)* the person to whom the words are addressed; or *(c)* a third person or group of persons overhearing the conversation.

Let us invent some thematic material and we shall see how the dramatic focus changes according to context.

1. *Recently the mother heard that Bobby Thompson was in trouble with the police because of drugs.* Thus as the daughter, unaware of this gossip, says, "But then I met Bobby Thompson there, and after it was over we went for a hamburger and a drive," the dramatic focus is on the mother, hearing it, rather than on the daughter, saying it. And so the director would probably film a close shot of the mother as she hears the words.
2. *The father must sign a crucial sales contract that week with Robert Thompson, Sr.—who took his son, Bobby, on a camping trip, and was supposed to be out of contact with anyone for two more weeks.* Now when the daughter says, "But then I met Bobby Thompson there . . . " the dramatic focus is on the father, to whom the girl is not even saying the words, and the director would obtain a close shot of him as he reacts to the news his daughter delivers so casually.
3. *With the girl in his car, Bobby Thompson had once driven recklessly, narrowly avoiding a serious accident, and she has been forbidden even to speak to him.* In this case, while the girl is telling how she not only spent time with Bobby at the party but also went with him for a drive in his car, the dramatic focus might be on her, as she delivers what amounts to a statement of defiance. But it also might be on either of her parents, or on both of them, depending upon what the story previously has established about their characterizations.

These examples, while somewhat melodramatic, do serve to plainly illustrate how the selection of camera angles is based on perceiving the dramatic focus of a scene, and then fulfilling the filmmaker's primary obligation—to give the audience what they would most like to see.

CAMERA SHOTS

It was suggested that a director might highlight the dramatic focus by way of a "close shot," which is a perfectly acceptable cinematic term, but not really a very specific one. There is, as we shall see, a whole repertoire of more precisely-named possibilities. Discussed first are the principal camera *shots,* which relate to the *purpose* of the angle of a shot; and then camera *moves,* relating to the *ways* of achieving a shot.

The Master Shot While all the shots to follow have their own distinctive uses, when used in the final construction of a scene they are often departures from some *master shot,* which is a basic utility shot containing all the main elements in a scene.

In our sample situation, the master shot would be made from a point at which the camera's view includes the mother, daughter, and father all the while that the scene's dialogue is spoken.

The highlighting of parts of the dialogue or action is left to additional shots, made separately, either from positions closer to the subjects or from particular angles, such as the points of view of various characters in the scene.

These other shots will later be used by the film editor as he or she cuts into the master shot to punctuate it with the various inserts. Sometimes half the footage of the master shot is replaced by insert shots. Sometimes the master shot is used intact, or perhaps with only one insert shot for a character's reaction. And sometimes the entire scene is a mosaic of insert shots, and the only visible remnant of the master shot is one small portion even shorter than the other shots.

The master shot is usually made first, for theoretically if an equipment malfunction should stop the shooting, or an earthquake occurs, or if one of the actors in a dramatic film suddenly becomes ill, the film can be produced using the master shot; while if a mishap occurs after two or three desired insert shots are filmed, but no master shot, the scene may not be able to be included in its entirety as scripted.

There are exceptions. For example, for a scene filmed at a factory, the master shot might be a wide view of all the activity in the main assembly area, with plans for additional closer shots of the various machines at work. But, as the film crew arrives, something especially interesting may be happening at one of the machines which will not soon happen again, and a number of close shots might first be made there, with the master shot being filmed afterwards.

Or, if one of the three actors in a scene is late on the set, the director might decide to start shooting the insert shots of the two actors who are present, instead of having the crew stand idle at full pay while they wait for the absent cast member to be included in the master shot of the scene.

A dramatic film whose scenes primarily consist of master shots, with few or no insert shots, has the somewhat static quality of a photographed stage play. A similarly shot industrial film has the visual effect of a series of posters. In both cases, the unique potential that film has for telling a story has been wasted.

The Establishing Shot The viewer of a film knows where and when things are happening by way of clues which the filmmaker provides. These clues come in the form of shots, and sometimes whole scenes, produced solely for the purpose.

The audience of any film may eventually become oriented without the aid of an establishing shot in a scene, *but this mental activity is precisely what the filmmaker wants to avoid.* A film cannot be put down for a few moments while the viewer mulls it over, for unlike the printed page the screen page inexorably keeps turning. Thus while the audience is occupied in puzzling out the locale of a scene, that scene and possibly others will go by without their full attention, and perhaps some subtlety which the filmmaker carefully planned will be irretrievably lost.

More important, the audience may reach a wrong conclusion which distorts the meaning of a key scene, and thereby misinterpret a crucial aspect of the entire film.

The business of establishing may go on all during a film, to inform the viewer where each scene is set. For example, a certain scene shows a man making a telephone call in an office. The style of the office may be irrelevant; what matters is that he is calling from an office and not from some other type of room. Thus the scene would not start with a close shot of the man, which tells the viewer nothing about where he is, but rather with a shot at least wide enough to reveal the desk and possibly a few file cabinets which clearly identify the room as a business office.

Once this establishing shot has accomplished its purpose, the film editor later will be able to vary the scene by inserting close shots of the man, shots of the person he is calling, or any other shots which the director may provide to build the scene.

If the scene is a short one, it may be filmed as one shot. If so, the shot would either remain wide for its duration, or start wide to establish before moving in closer to get the full impact of what the man is saying into the telephone.

Even though a scene's setting has been established, it later may be re-established to remind the viewer. This depends on how many times it occurs in the film, and how much time elapses between its appearances. But even if the recurrent scene is not always preceded by a special establishing shot, the first shot of the scene itself will usually be wide enough to establish it.

Many scenes require more than one establishing shot. For example, before we are introduced to a significant character who lives in a rundown section of a Western town, we first will see a broad shot of the landscape, which establishes "the West," followed by a shot of the town; then a shot of the neighborhood, to establish "rundown"; then a shot of the exterior of the house; and only then will we see the character in the interior of her house.

If we come back to her within a reasonably short time, she could be shown solely in a close shot without confusing the audience as to her location. If more time elapses before we return to her, a brief shot of the exterior of her house would precede the scene.

An establishing shot usually serves its purpose best when it comes early in a scene, but there are occasions when it is purposely delayed to achieve a particular effect. A familiar example might be a scene showing a young man in a close shot at the head of a boardroom conference table, as he tells why he thinks he deserves a promotion. Then an establishing shot reveals that he is in fact alone in the room, wistfully rehearsing.

Another example, accomplishing an opposite effect, was seen in a television commercial which opened on a shot of a girl sunning herself on a pool-side lounge, ostensibly in complete privacy; then the establishing shot, made with the camera on a crane, widened to reveal that she actually was one of a hundred or more bodies crowded around a huge pool at a resort hotel.

An establishing shot may be used to establish time as well as place. For example, if our office telephoner is first shown entering his office carrying a newspaper and a container of coffee, which he sets down and then opens after hanging up his jacket, we know it is morning. If his telephone call is preceded by a shot of the corridor outside his office being mopped by a janitor, we know it is late at night.

The filmmaker and the film editor, in their respective ways, see to it that each establishing shot seems to belong where it is so naturally that the viewer never appreciates it for what it is, like those familiar amenities in everyday life which are noticed only when they are not there.

Reaction and Cutaway Shots A reaction shot, obviously, is one that shows somebody reacting to something that is said or done. What is not so apparent, however, is the great versatility of this shot, for it can also be useful in ways not necessarily related to reactions. But first let us consider how the reaction shot is used *as* a reaction shot.

As seen in our discussion of dramatic focus, the *effect* of things that are said or done is often more interesting than the saying or doing of them. Thus a director will often plan special insert shots designed to capture specific reactions. He or she may decide in advance on one particular kind, and shoot only that one; or a variety of possible reaction shots may be filmed, with the final selection left for the editing stage.

For example, in our sample scene, if the reaction to be shown is that of the father as he hears in his daughter's casual chatter the item of news so important to his business, the director might shoot the following, after making the master shot:

1. A wide shot of the father from the daughter's point of view, as he listens to the entire conversation, so that the editor may cut to a shot or two of the father apparently not interested in what is being said until the significant point, thus heightening the impact of his eventual reaction.
2. A shot of the daughter from the father's point of view as she delivers her lines, so that the editor may cut from a closeup of the father, as he hears the first mention of Bobby Thompson's name, to an angle representing what he sees as he looks at her when she tells about meeting the boy.

With these shots, in addition to the master shot, the editor has an opportunity to construct the scene in the most effective way possible. If it is an important scene, the editor, working with the director, may build the scene a number of different ways until the final combination of master shot and insert shots is approved.

In theatrical films, every exchange of dialogue, except the most minor kind, is often filmed at least three ways.

For example, in our sample scene, after the master shot has been made, the actress playing the mother would be filmed in a close shot as she delivers all of her lines to the camera, against the reading of the daughter's dialogue by a staff member on the other side of the camera, which is later cut out. Then the actress would be filmed in closeup as she listens, and reacts, to the daughter's lines read by the staff member.

The actress playing the daughter would do the same.

And so the exchange between mother and daughter would be built from a combination of master shot, mother's close dialogue shots, mother's close reaction shots, daughter's close dialogue shots, daughter's close reaction shots, and father's reaction shots.

This procedure illustrates the tremendous creative control which is possible in film production. It also reveals the potential tedium so inherent in theatrical filmmaking—which explains why some actors seem to give an uneven performance in certain scenes of a movie. They may have burned with dramatic intensity during the shooting of the master shot—when they were actually playing to the other actors in the scene—but cooled down just a bit during the filming of their separate close shots, when they were playing to a camera lens and an anonymous line reader. But the film editor has built the scene with portions of both filming sessions, and therefore shots of the actors which appear within seconds of each other on the screen may actually have been filmed hours or even days apart.

Although reaction shots are effective when used as such, they also are most useful as *cutaway shots.* The function of a cutaway shot is better illustrated than explained:

A film editor has a shot of a man talking continuously for two minutes. The shot must be shortened by fifteen seconds. But the unwanted fifteen seconds of talk is located in the middle of the shot.

Because the shot is *continuous,* if the editor cuts out the unwanted piece in the middle, the man will seem to make an unnatural movement—for example, one moment his head is turned to the left as he smiles, and the very next instant his head is abruptly turned to the right and he has no smile. The reason it would be so jarring is that the viewer, thinking the action is continuous, could not account for the odd jerkiness or jump.

The solution is simple: the mismatch will not be apparent if the frames of picture on either side of the cut are separated from each other by the insertion of some other shot between them, which briefly cuts away from the original shot.

Since an essential requirement for a cutaway shot is that it appear *logical* as an insert, a reaction shot is ideal when editing a shot of somebody talking. Documentary filmmakers and television newsfilm crews, when filming an interview in or out of the studio, routinely film a lengthy shot of the interviewer or reporter as he or she listens with interest to the interviewee's answers. This footage later proves valuable as the source of cutaway shots which enable the editor to quickly and easily chop the interviewee's answers down to any required length.

It is, in fact, common practice for an on-camera reporter or interviewer to be filmed for this purpose as he or she "listens with interest" long before or after the interview actually takes place.

But, of course, shots of people talking are not the only ones which have to be edited in the middle, and filmmakers must shoot suitable cutaways for every significant shot—or they may find that some over-long favorite, which cannot logically be trimmed at its beginning or end, looked marvelous in the camera but will never reach the screen.

POV and Reverse Angle Shots POV is an acronym for the phrase "point of view," used in connection with what the camera "sees" from a particular person's point of view.

A specialized form of the POV shot is the *reverse angle shot.* As the name indicates, this is a shot filmed from exactly the reverse of the angle of whatever shot preceded it. A familiar example is in the scene of a man walking along a corridor and approaching a door. He rings the bell. The door is opened by a woman, whom we see in the doorway. The next shot abruptly reverses our angle of view by 180°: we now see the man in the corridor from the woman's POV.

Another familiar reverse angle shot is popular with the makers of television commercials. First we see a person opening their refrigerator door. Then a reverse angle shows the person peering in at us through the open door, as though the camera were now positioned in the butter dish.

The Closeup The closeup has two basic functions. The first is utilitarian: to enlarge a subject which otherwise would appear on the screen too small to be studied. The second is expressive: to isolate a subject on the screen and thereby highlight it.

The first use of the closeup is so plainly practical that once it has been defined it has been discussed. Let us therefore concern ourselves primarily with the second function of the closeup, as an expressive device.

No shot is so overused and misused as this one. Ideally, a closeup should be on film what italics are in print—a conveyor of emphasis or special significance. But *when many words* in *a* sentence *are italicized, as* in this *one, no one word in the sentence can* have *any special* impact. The same holds true when many shots in a scene are closeups.

Consequently, filmmakers who indiscriminately fill their work with closeups find that when they want a particular shot to bear the burden of emphasis they must use something else to arrest the viewer's attention. These often are odder and odder camera angles, until ultimately the camera imparts distortion and confusion to shots intended to be especially meaningful.

There are two basic types of closeup, representing two degrees of closeness of the subject on the screen. Their definitions are less than precise, for the exact dimension of any closeup depends on the subject, the cinematographer, and the purpose of the shot.

To identify the two types we shall apply them, according to

generally accepted professional use, to a shot of a man sitting in a chair, facing us.

A *closeup* (CU) would fill the screen with his head and little more. The top of the frame would just clear or slightly crop his hair, and the bottom frame would go no further down than the knot of his necktie.

An *extreme closeup* (ECU, or more informally, BCU for "big closeup") would fill the screen with a shot of his face from his eyebrows to the top of his chin just below his lower lip. This view, from eyebrows down to mouth, is probably the closest the average cinematographer would go in framing a shot scripted as ECU—WAYNE. To go in closer would usually require a more specific instruction, such as ECU—WAYNE'S EYES, etc.

The closeup requires some care not only in its aesthetic use by the director and film editor, but also in its technical use by the cinematographer. A camera shooting through a normal lens will distort the perspective of any object to which it gets too close. Competent camera operators know the limits of the lens they are using, and when necessary will change to one of proper focal length for shooting a particular closeup.

However, the fact that a camera lens will distort images when used too close can be used for creative purposes. This effect can be achieved either openly or subtly; the former is more likely to call attention to the filmmaker's cleverness, but the latter is more apt to accomplish the objective.

CAMERA MOVES

The quality of any film rises in proportion to how free the camera is to contribute movement of its own, instead of only being allowed to record the movement of other things. There are two reasons for this.

One is that camera movement during a shot, when it is warranted, is of course more interesting than a static view. The key words here are "when it is warranted"; like all good things, it can be overdone. In *Film and Its Techniques,* one of the best books ever written on the technical aspects of documentary film production, the late Raymond Spottiswoode wrote:

> *In revolt against the dead and empty shots of some conventional directors and cameramen, there has been a recent tendency to demand that every shot in a film be packed with action. As a result, most shots in information films have people walking in from the left, running by*

> *from the right, and circulating around in all parts of the shot not otherwise occupied with movement. This artificial frenzy is often dignified with the term "planes of action." In reality, it is the significance and not the quantity of action which determines the success of a shot. A single lifted finger may be more dramatic than a skyful of airplanes.**

The other reason is somewhat more subtle. The realism of motion pictures is not due solely to the novelty of seeing subjects moving in the picture. In addition, when the camera itself moves, giving the audience the experience of passing various objects on different planes, it overcomes the basic photographic limitation of showing the world in only two dimensions on a flat screen, by imparting an illusion of depth.

All camera moves require some care in execution, for as soon as a motion picture camera is moved while it is operating, the laws of optics are invoked, and each camera move will be seen to have its own particular problem in not transgressing one of these laws.

Panning and Tilting The most simple move that can be made with a camera is merely to swing it horizontally from left to right or vice versa. Such a move made while the camera is running is called a *pan,* a shortening of its original name, *panorama shot.* A pan may be brief—panning from bride to groom as they stand together at the altar—or it may indeed be panoramic as it sweeps the entire skyline of a great city.

The basic reasons for panning, as with most camera moves, are to follow some movement on the part of the subject, or to more fully show something which is too large to be completely seen from one angle. However, it is when camera movement is unrelated to these practical chores that creativity becomes involved, for then the camera's movement is designed to be aesthetically interesting, or more significantly, to make a cinematic statement of its own.

This statement may consist of a special emphasis given to the relationship between two points of interest, such as a man who is being pursued on a city street and a cruising taxi which could be his means of escape. The relationship between the two could very well be indicated by a shot of the man, followed by a shot of the taxi. But a single shot that pans from the man to the taxi establishes the relationship more pointedly, even urgently, for it takes the viewer's eye from one to the other in a direct and continuous path.

*Raymond Spottiswoode, *Film and Its Techniques* (Berkeley and Los Angeles: University of California Press, 1970), p. 30.

Similarly, a pan may evoke a physical sensation, such as in a scene showing a woman within reach of an object she is anxious, or fearful, to touch, because the pan represents the actual path the woman's hand would travel if she were to reach for the object.

The decision to pan must be carefully considered in relation to its place in the scene, for once begun, a pan generally must be permitted to complete its course without interruption. This is because the usual techniques of cutting away to another shot then coming back, or ending the scene, cannot be used during a pan, for it would be visually unsettling when seen on the screen.

A prime requirement of a pan is that it be perfectly smooth. No matter how "acceptable" a little shakiness appears through the camera's eyepiece during a pan, the shot will usually prove to be unusable when later seen projected on a screen.

However, a more important—in fact, essential—requirement is that *pans must be relatively slow moves,* the camera ideally moving no faster than about half the speed envisioned for the pan on the screen. The reason for this is an interesting one, involving the illusory nature of the "motion" in motion pictures.

It is a physiological effect known as *persistence of vision* which causes our eyes to see the frames of film not as the series of slightly different still photographs that they are, but as an illusion of continuous motion.

But while persistence of vision produces the illusion in cinematography that a still body is moving, it is also known to scientists in another field, the study of light, as the cause of precisely the *opposite* illusion, whereby a moving body appears to be motionless—for it has been observed that when a fast-moving object, such as a whirling pinwheel, is bathed in a bright enough saturation of light for a brief enough interval, it will appear to freeze in its motion for that moment. This is known as a *stroboscopic effect.*

These two contrasting illusions confront each other any time that a panning movie camera, or its subject, moves too fast. When this occurs, the stroboscopic effect, familiarly called "strobing," causes the frames of film to lose their guise of continuous motion and instead be clearly seen as the individual still photographs they are, as they skip by in a characteristic streaking motion.

If a pan is *extremely* fast it will result, not in strobing, but in a plain, old-fashioned blur. Sometimes just such a blur will be purposely caused, for use as a vivid transitional device between scenes, usually a horizontally moving blur of bright colored lights shot at night. This effect is called a *swish pan,* presumably because the lights, or whatever is being panned, whip by so fast that one can almost hear the swish. When used appropriately by a film editor, a swish pan is a very effective device for dramatically punctuating the end of a scene, or for establishing a breathless tempo in a particular sequence.*

The cousin of the pan is the *tilt:* the camera pans the row of houses, but it tilts up the rocket on the gantry.

Although tilting might seem merely to be the vertical equivalent of panning, it is not, for the cinematic opportunities, as well as the optical problems, are different.

In tilting, a marked distortion of perspective occurs when the camera is close to its subject, and the distortion increases in proportion to the closeness. Thus a man of normal size appears to be a towering giant when the camera is positioned at his feet and tilts up to his head. Conversely, the same man looks quite small when the camera is placed slightly above him and tilts down.

Cinematographers wishing to make an undistorted tilting shot of a subject must back away until their eyepiece and experience tell them that they have reached the right distance.

This distance, which varies with each subject's size and shape, marks the photographic dividing line between truth and tampering with the truth. Cinematographers and directors contemplating a tilting shot are often tempted to embellish reality for aesthetic reasons, for example tilting up a mountain at an angle from which it may appear more majestic than it actually is. On other occasions the line between photographic truth and falsity is crossed for more practical reasons—to make a car's grille appear more massive in a television commercial, or to make a short actor look as tall as he is popularly imagined to be.

The Dolly Shot When a camera is moved along the surface on a conveyance while it is shooting, it is said to *dolly:* OPEN ON WIDE SHOT OF CROWDED WEDDING CHAPEL, THEN DOLLY IN FOR CLOSE SHOT OF BRIDE AND GROOM AT ALTAR.

The dolly itself may be any vehicle on which the camera is riding during a shot. Thus a dolly can be one of the elaborate mobile platforms built specifically for the purpose and used in major motion picture production, or it can be some child's little red wagon temporarily pressed into service by a documentary film producer in the field.

*Scene transitions are discussed in Chapter 8, *The Editing of Film.*

Dolly shot actually refers to a family of camera moves, many of which have more specific names, depending upon what path the camera takes while riding on the dolly.

When the camera travels along with its subject, keeping the camera-to-subject distance constant, it may be called a *travelling shot,* as when the camera follows a person as he or she walks along the street. An alternate name sometimes used for this shot, as well as for when the camera moves along a street or a store aisle without relating to any one particular person, is a *trucking shot.*

Another name, *tracking shot,* once referred specifically to those moving shots made while the camera dolly rides on special tracks, or rails, to ensure absolute smoothness and control; today *tracking* is often used as an omnibus term for all dolly shots, particularly those that follow, or "track," a subject.

The dolly shots most often encountered in day-to-day film production entail moving the camera *toward* and *away from* a subject: DOLLY IN ON TELEPHONE AS IT RINGS or DOLLY BACK TO REVEAL JASON'S DOG LYING AT HIS FEET.

Dollying in and dollying back may sometimes present some technical considerations, and the filmmaker who is aware of them will be able to more intelligently plan a shooting schedule. The laws of optics state that when camera-to-subject distance changes, the camera focus generally has to be readjusted. Dollying in or out, of course, causes the camera-to-subject distance to change continually, hence the focal setting of the camera lens must be changed a number of times during the move. This is known as *follow focus.*

Ideally, the cinematographer should be allotted some time in which to plan a long dolly shot with an assistant, so that at prearranged points along the route the assistant may change the focal setting of the lens to preselected positions. In this way, the cinematographer can fully concentrate on achieving smooth movement and correct framing.

The Zoom Another method of moving into or away from a subject is by use of the *zoom,* in which the effect of movement is simulated optically by means of a special lens, while the camera never actually moves.

"Zooming in," as even the phrase itself indicates, can be more dramatic than dollying—but there are disadvantages to a zoom which must be considered before choosing it over the less spectacular dolly shot. To understand the relative merits, let us examine what a zoom lens is and what it does.

The author preparing for a shot with a zoom lens on a 35mm camera.

A zoom lens is specially designed so that it is able to vary the focal length, from close to far and everywhere in between, while keeping the image constantly in focus.*

To accomplish this, the lens system is a complex one, and because of all the complicated optical engineering in them, zoom lenses generally must sacrifice some photographic quality for their unique capabilities.

This relative loss of picture quality varies from negligible to noticeable, depending on the individual lens, the cinematographer using it, and the details of the shot. But it is outweighed by the merits of the lens when it provides its characteristic *z-o-o-m,* with all the vivid impact the move contributes to a shot.

*This does not conflict with the optical principle that a camera's focus must be changed when the camera-to-subject distance changes, because the distance between camera and subject here does *not* actually change; it only *seems* to do so.

When the zoom lens is used in a slow move, as a kind of "lazy man's dolly," the interests of the audience are not always served, for a dolly shot will show more depth than a zoom shot.

Remember, the "closeness" is but an illusion; the reality is that the camera lens remains far from the subject scene, with the optical significance such distance entails. In a dolly shot, however, the camera lens *is* brought close to the subject scene, and consequently the perspective retains all the depth that the particular lens can reflect.

This, of course, presents little problem in choice when the desired effect is the dramatic "zeroing in" of the zoom shot, whether across a table or across a town. But when the objective is simply a normal moving shot across a room, for example, a slowly-cranked zoom is no true substitute for a dolly shot.

This is because in a dolly shot the camera (the eye of the audience) passes a lamp, a table, some chairs, etc., on its way to the subject, thus providing the familiar sense of depth which one experiences in natural motion. But in the zoom shot, the audience would not experience a feeling of moving past things as they approached the subject, for what happens in a zoom is that the subject is actually being enlarged, with the surrounding area thus being gradually cropped out, bringing the subject to the viewer in a kind of visual tunnel.

THE SHOOTING/EDITING RELATIONSHIP

The best footage is shot, and the best films are produced, by filmmakers who are aware of the blood kinship between shooting and editing.

First, as a practical consideration, most directors and field producers, when later working at the side of a film editor, have sometimes fruitlessly searched the rolls of film for a certain kind of shot to cover a particular line in the narration, or one to be used in relation to other shots to accomplish an important dramatic effect in a scene. Since the editing often takes place after all the shooting has been completed and the cast and crew have long been dismissed, if that desirable shot is not there it represents an oversight while filming that is impossible to remedy.

Just as important is the creative aspect. When shooting, it is a mistake to think only of making good individual shots. Remember: *no single shot appears alone in a film; its ultimate effect is in its on-screen relationship to other shots.*

Really inspired camera work can usually survive a certain amount of butchery in the cutting room, and creative editing can often make bad film look acceptable. However, when shooting and editing are not considered as separate steps of film production, but rather as the two parts of a dual process, then might the film cross the line beyond which craft becomes art.

SHOOTING SOUND ON FILM

Since our perception of the world around us primarily is through two of our five senses—sight and sound—no film can attain the illusion of reality which every filmmaker seeks without presenting both picture and sound with equal skill.

SYNCHRONOUS SOUND

All the different sounds involved in a film's production primarily are divided into two types: synchronous and nonsynchronous.

If the recording of the sound is directly linked to the camera *during filming,* it is synchronous sound, often shortened to "sync." If it has been recorded any other way, it is nonsynchronous or *wild sound.*

Some common examples of wild sound include narration, music and sound effects recorded separately in a sound studio.

Wild sound may later be aligned with some specific action on the screen, in *postsynchronization.*

For example, on the screen we see a man firing a gun and simultaneously hear the sound of the shot. In traditional movie or television filming, that gunshot may be dubbed in, days or even weeks later, as a sound effect.* But because a film editor inserted the sound so precisely against the picture, and a sound engineer later applied exactly the right volume at exactly the right moment during a sound mixing session, the firing of the gun and the sound of the shot are as perfectly "in sync" as though they had actually happened simultaneously on the set during filming.

Another example of postsynchronization is the method often used to record dialogue for a scene being shot away from the studio, on location.

Dialogue is the primary sound in most theatrical films, and therefore much effort and technology are employed to always record it at the optimal level of quality. However, the synchronous recording of dialogue on a location set is often limited by two factors. First, some portable sound equipment is not equal technically to the equipment installed in a studio. Then, even though a location unit may bring sound equipment that *is* as good as that found in a studio, they cannot bring the studio: the location area itself is more frequently the problem.

One solution is to have the actors speak their lines while the camera turns as usual, but with no sound being recorded; then later, in a fully-equipped recording studio, the same actors repeat the lines while watching their scenes being projected on a screen, until they attain satisfactory synchronization.

Since few scenes are shot without some minor deviation from the scripted lines, it is necessary to have a record of exactly which words, in what order, the actors did say during the filming of the location scene, so that synchronization between mouth and words, familiarly called *lip sync,* may be achieved in the dubbing session.

This is often accomplished by a staff member carefully noting any variations from the script during the filming, then making a revised script of that scene for use at the dubbing session. A better method is to have notes made, but also record the dialogue while filming with no attempt at any sound quality beyond mere intelligibility. This recording, called a *guide track* or *scratch track,* is preferable to the stenographic record alone because it not only guides the actors in what they said, but in exactly how they said it.

Although the same technique is possible in the case of an on-camera narrator in a problem location setting, it is seldom necessary, because narration easily can be studio recorded to start with, and used as voice-over-film for that scene.

*The reasons for this are discussed in Chapter 10, *Sound Effects On Film.*

A 35mm camera for non-synchronous filming (silent footage). (Courtesy of Arriflex Corp.)

Location scenes may also be shot without sound for reasons unrelated to recording problems.

For example, a scene's actual sound may not be significant enough to warrant the use of sound equipment during its filming, such as a high, sweeping view of some beautiful natural scenery. Thus it would appear without any specific sound, except perhaps the general background music of the film.

Or a scene may have sound that *is* significant, such as the noise of a factory or the din of a busy downtown street, but not so unique that suitable sound effects cannot be dubbed in later, involving less bother and expense during the filming.

While in almost any filming situation a filmmaker may or may not decide to shoot silent footage and later match it to wild sound, some subjects obviously call for synchronous shooting. The most familiar example of this is lip sync (the lack of which is usually the most noticeable sign to the average viewer that a film is "out of sync"), such as dialogue or on-camera narration.

Single-system Versus Double-system Once it has been decided that a scene will be filmed with synchronous sound, two different methods of achieving this are available—*single-system* and *double-system*. Before examining how each method accomplishes what is required, let us briefly consider just what these requirements are.

In professional sound filming, the picture is recorded at a constant rate of exactly twenty-four frames of film per second, called *sound speed,* which results in what we perceive as natural motion when seen on the screen. No shot is ready to be made until there is confirmation (by calling out "Speed!" to the director in traditional Hollywood shooting) that the camera and sound recorder are running at sound speed.

To ensure filming at true sound speed, a professional cinematographer uses a camera equipped with a special synchronous motor, which is designed to continually respond to any fluctuations in the frequency of the electrical power supply by adjusting the speed of the camera to compensate, thus keeping the camera drive operating at a constant rate of twenty-four frames per second.

However, in synchronous filming, it would be of little use for the picture to be dutifully filmed at sound speed *if* the sound were being recorded at some other speed. For then, what later appeared on the screen inevitably would be "out of sync"—because, for example, while the saying of "I love you. . ." was shot to run two seconds on film, it was recorded to run only one and a half seconds on the sound track, or vice versa.

The necessity, then, in synchronous filming, is that the picture and sound not only be recorded simultaneously, but also that they both be recorded at the same prescribed speed.*

In the *single-system* method, which is not available in 35mm, the camera does both jobs. The microphone is connected to the camera, which simultaneously records both picture and sound on the same piece of special film, often called "stripe film" or simply "stripe," because of the thin strip of magnetic recording film running along one side of it.† The picture and sound are thus locked into synchronization on the film itself.

In *double-system,* the camera shoots only the picture, and the sound is simultaneously recorded separately, usually by a specially-equipped tape recorder. (It is possible to use a second camera to record only the sound, instead of a tape recorder, but the practice is relatively rare.)

Synchronization of the camera and the tape recorder may be ensured by the use of a *sync pulse generator,* a device inside the

*When film sound is recorded wild, for later synchronization to picture, steps are taken in the studio or in the field to ensure that the sound is recorded and will play back exactly at sound speed.

† Earlier in single-system filming, an optical track was recorded on the film. With the development of magnetic recording film and tape, optical recording has fallen into disuse. However, some cameras that record optically, and the film to go with them, still survive.

A 35mm studio camera used for synchronous filming of feature motion pictures. (Courtesy of Panavision, Inc.)

camera, or attached to its motor, which sends a constant "true sync speed" reference signal to the tape recorder, by which special circuits in the recorder regulate its tape speed to match that of the camera. This may be accomplished by way of a cable between camera and tape recorder, the standard procedure for many years, or by a comparatively newer, cable-free method of transmitting the sync pulse via wireless radio signal.

However, another way of synchronizing the camera and the recorder, even more convenient than the wireless radio method, is popularly known as "crystal sync." This involves the use of individual crystal-controlled oscillators on both camera and recorder, which

A 16mm camera used for double-system synchronous filming in the studio or the field. (Courtesy of Arriflex Corp.)

hold them in synchronization without cables or radio signals between them.*

The result of all this gadgetry will be synchronization of the sound and the picture during filming, as desired—but then what? Since it is double-system, in reality the sound is on a reel of magnetic tape but the picture is on a roll of film—two physically separate entities. It's all very well to say that, technically, sound and picture are "synchronized," but since they are separated, how does one know exactly which frame of film relates to which fraction of an inch of sound track?

Amidst all the complicated technology, the answer often is the simple manual act of banging two sticks together—the function of the *clapstick slate.*

Before a shot is made for almost any type of professional filming, a member of the production staff holds a slate in front of the camera once it has come up to speed, showing at least the following information: the number of the shot or scene according to the script; which "take," or attempt at an acceptable shot, is about to be filmed;

*A handy improvisational technique for filming synchronous sound when a camera is not equipped with any kind of sync pulse generator is discussed later in this chapter, in *Film Sound Recorders.*

the date; the film's title or production number, if any; the names of the camera operator and the director; and whether the locale is interior or exterior. Later, when the film editor picks up that roll of film, a glance at the first few frames immediately identifies the scene that follows.

However, if the filming is in double-system synchronous sound, the slate will be the clapstick type—meaning that its top will consist of two strips of hardwood, painted with diagonal black and white stripes for maximum visibility and joined by a hinge at one end. With the camera rolling and the sound being recorded, the staff member holding the slate calls out the basic scene identification, then raises the top strip of the slate and briskly brings it down against the bottom strip with a sharp, loud *clack.*

Later, when looking at the beginning of that roll, the film editor will mark the one frame in which the clapsticks first come together; on the sound track the editor will hear the resultant *clack,* which is

The author using a clapstick slate, for double-system filming of on-camera narration by NBC correspondent Frank McGee, inside the Johnson Space Center in Houston prior to the *Apollo 11* moon landing mission.

also marked. Thus, by simply lining up the marked frame with the mark on the track, the sound and picture of that shot can easily and accurately be brought "into sync" at any time during the ensuing production process.

While the hand-held clapstick slate is a standard method of slating, widely used in professional film production, some cameras have a built-in slating system, requiring a cable to the tape recorder. When the camera reaches sound speed, it automatically turns a small interior light on and off to fog a few frames of film, simultaneously transmitting a *beep* which is received and taped by the recorder. This is especially useful for synchronous filming of intermittent action that happens each time with little or no warning.

However, the standard procedure for shooting sound film quickly without first using a slate is *tail slating,* whereby the camera and tape recorder keep running after the desired shot has been made, long enough for a proper clapstick slating. The editor then synchronizes the film and track from the tail of the scene instead of from the head.

And still another method, used by film crews as an emergency measure (and by many low-budget units as standard procedure), is the least complicated of all. The technique is simple: you just hold the microphone in front of the camera and hit it with your hand.

Between single-system and double-system filming, double-system is overwhelmingly preferred and most widely used by professional film producers today.

This might appear to be an interesting example of mass perversity, for single-system would seem obviously to be the surer and easier method. Surer, because the synchronized sound and picture are safely locked onto the same piece of film. Easier, because far less equipage is involved, as evidenced by the fact that it took only one short paragraph to describe, compared to the eleven which double-system required.

However, the paradox is more apparent than real, for experience would show that, as usual, there are trade-offs involved, and the advantages are worth the trade only to a specialized few.

Because single-system is less cumbersome to use and faster to process, it is favored primarily by camera crews who are out shooting film for the six o'clock news, and others who similarly need maximum speed and mobility more than optimal quality.

In single-system, two complex jobs, of camera and tape recorder, must both be accomplished within the limited confines of one standard-sized piece of equipment, the inevitable result being something of a compromise in each function, especially in the sound recording.

The recording device in single-system necessarily is small, to fit its somewhat cramped quarters, and the strip it records on is a narrow one-tenth of an inch in width. In comparison, the recording equipment used in double-system, being completely separate, can be as complex and of as high a quality as the budget allows, recording on tape from a quarter-inch to a full inch in width, for optimum dynamic range.

In addition, single-system is decidedly less convenient to edit. On the stripe film used in single-system, the sound always precedes its corresponding picture by twenty-eight frames, to accommodate the physical separation of the playback head and the film gate and lamp in a projector. Thus, without specialized equipment found in some television news departments but not in the typical cutting room, a film editor working with 16mm stripe cannot cut picture and sound together at any desired place.

This means that if you want to start a shot with a man saying some specific words, the film must be cut twenty-eight frames earlier than his mouth is seen to form the words, which is where those words are on the sound track. This is why shots of people being interviewed at the scene of some news story on television often show lips moving with no sound for the first one and one-sixth seconds.

Except for news film which must go on the air quickly, single-system footage is often sent to a sound studio to have the sound on the strip of magnetic film made into a separate track, for conventional editing and later mixing of picture and sound. However, if sound and picture are subsequently to be worked on as separate entities, as usual, there is little point to shooting in single-system, with its lesser sound quality, in the first place.

SOUND EQUIPMENT ON THE SET

Each new issue of the film equipment catalogs brings news of highly specialized items of equipment which can perform marvelous feats that the familiar workhorses of everyday production cannot do. They are devilishly useful—especially for that special problem which only they can solve—but no stern-faced production manager would permit their inclusion in the budget as standard equipment. Thus, on the film set as in the automobile showroom, once you go beyond the basic requirements, what is "necessary" very much depends on individual needs and financial means.

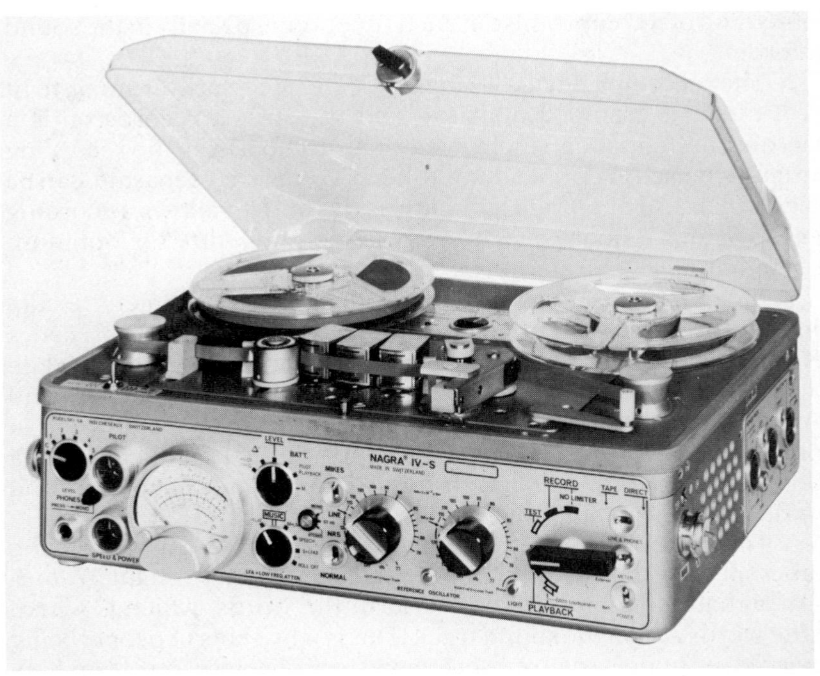

A fully equipped recorder for use in taping synchronous sound while filming in the studio or the field. (Courtesy of Nagra Magnetic Recorders, Inc.)

Let us therefore concern ourselves with basic sound equipment, used by a typical filmmaker whose budget is midway between shoestring and carte blanche.

Film Sound Recorders As with most electronic equipment, tape recorders for use in double-system filming vary in their capabilities, depending upon cost. However, any tape recorder to be used in recording film sound should at least have the ability to record and play two tracks—one for the sound being recorded, and one for a sync signal to regulate the recorder's speed to that of the camera.

High-quality tape machines designed for use in professional filmmaking, such as the Nagra, Perfectone and Rangertone, all are specially equipped to utilize a sync pulse signal.

However, if necessary, any fairly good tape recorder designed to play and record in stereo (which is two-track) can be adapted by a technician for use in a "homemade" version of double-system sound recording, which makes use of the fact that A.C. (Alternating

Current) cycles on and off sixty times each second, unlike D.C. (Direct Current) which flows continuously.

In this procedure it is possible to use a camera that is not equipped with a sync pulse generator. Instead, the tape machine's second channel is fed a sufficient amount of ordinary sixty-cycle A.C. electricity from a power source, thereby recording a pulse signal which later may be used as a reference for synchronization. However, in order for this reference to be valid, the camera must have an A.C. synchronous motor and receive its electrical power from the same A.C. source used by the recorder, so that any fluctuations in power during filming will affect recorder and camera identically.

This technique's dependence on the use of A.C. current is seldom a problem when shooting and recording in a studio or other indoor location, where sixty-cycle A.C. current usually is available. In the field, however, the use of A.C. power, instead of the D.C. current provided by the batteries in most portable equipment, could entail the cost and encumbrance of special storage batteries, electric current converters and motor controls, which might decrease the advantage of using the less expensive tape recorder and camera outdoors.

Among machines designed more specifically for professional film sound recording, there are some models equipped to record directly onto 16mm or 35mm magnetic sound film, which offers a potential for better sound quality in the original recording. Most models, however, use conventional quarter-inch magnetic tape, which is less expensive, more readily available far from specialized sources, and generally involves equipment that is more easily portable.

Features found on better tape recorders—VU meters to provide visual measurement of sound levels, separate recording and playback heads, increased tape load capacity, etc.—are always desirable, and sometimes necessary, depending upon the individual filming project.

Other features may fill a specialized need, such as dual microphone inputs, with separate volume controls, if two microphones will be required during some of the filming. Recording with more than two microphones usually requires the use of a *mixer,* a unit in which the incoming signals are combined, adjusted for volume level and balance, and passed along to the recorder.

Two features, however, can prove to be consistently useful in almost any synchronous filming situation: headphone monitoring and choice of tape speed.

Headphone Monitoring. Almost every tape recorder has a small speaker, usually of utilitarian quality, primarily designed to permit listening to what has already been recorded. For professional results, however, it is important to be able to accurately monitor the sound *while* it is being recorded.

Ideally, for this purpose, the recorder should be isolated from the sound source and hooked into a good speaker system, as may be possible inside a film studio or outdoors using a special mobile sound unit. However, since the ideal is not always within range of the average film production budget, professional monitoring of sound while filming is very often accomplished by the use of headphones.

Even if for no other reason, monitoring can simply confirm that the sound entering the recorder is, in fact, of acceptable quality. I recall a number of filming sessions which would have been impossible to repeat if something went wrong—such as when my crew was teetering on the edge of a Virginia rooftop overlooking the Pentagon, or at Cape Kennedy just before a launch—which were saved from being shot with sound that was not broadcast quality, by the recordist hearing it in his headphones and quickly hunting down an unnoticed loose cable.

The basic function of monitoring is to permit constant control of the sound levels being recorded. Even with a machine that has no operative VU meters, an experienced recordist, using headphones, can make such judgments subjectively. In addition, he or she can be alerted to the need to move a microphone during filming—for example, further from the sound source if the onset of distortion is detected, or closer if background noise starts to encroach. (Moving the microphone only twenty-five percent closer to the subject can result in a two hundred percent drop in unwanted background noise.)

The selection of headphones should be made carefully. For example, it is important that they fit properly enough to avoid the distraction of discomfort, no matter how slight, while subtle decisions on sound level are being made. More important, they must effectively screen the recordist's ears, so there is no problem in differentiating between the sound as it comes from its source, live, and the sound as it is being recorded.

While headphones of low quality make evaluation of recorded sound difficult or even impossible, in this case it could be just as unwise to select headphones that are too good, or at least better than they have to be. If the film for which the sound is being recorded is 16mm, the optical sound track on the final composite print will have specific limitations both in frequency response and dynamic range. The rich fullness of a singer's higher tones, clearly heard through high fidelity headphones, may not be there when heard from the screen on 16mm sound track, which cannot faithfully reproduce those higher tones.

Therefore, why not hear the sound through headphones whose capacity more closely resembles that of a film's sound track? That way, what sounds good in the recordist's ear will probably sound good in the completed film.

Choice of Tape Speed. While almost all portable open-reel (non-cassette) tape recorders in general use are equipped to record at 7½ i.p.s.,* many models designed for professional work can also record at the faster 15 i.p.s., the tape speed used in most studio recording sessions, which provides far better sound reproduction and the potential for more comprehensive editing. Recordings of voices talking, or of various sounds in a scene, can often be satisfactorily taped at 7½ i.p.s., but if music is to be recorded (as anything but one of the incidental background sounds) the higher tape speed is considered essential by most professional recordists.

Microphones Microphones differ in their *acceptance angles,* which is the shape of the sound pattern they are designed to "hear." There are three types most suitable for use in recording film sound.

Omnidirectional microphones have an acceptance angle of approximately 300 degrees, to record sound coming to them from any direction except directly behind them. Although this relatively unrestricted recording pattern has made them the most popular type of microphone in general nonprofessional use, they are less popular with filmmakers, who usually want more selective control of what will be recorded.

Ultradirectional microphones, also called *unidirectional,* record sound from only one direction, a narrow forty-degree cone-shaped area directly in front of them. Often called "shotgun mikes," they are particularly useful in picking out specific sounds from among many in an area, such as isolating one person's speech from the general din around him or her in a noisy crowd.

Cardioid microphones have an acceptance pattern that makes them especially desirable for most filming situations. It is an angle of approximately eighty degrees, but in a somewhat heart-shaped pattern—designed to most clearly pick up sounds in front of them, but also, to a lesser degree, from either side. This permits a more

*Inches per second.

natural mixture of specific sound plus some peripheral sound around it.

Within these basic types,* microphones have different ranges of frequency response, which describes the scope of the instrument's ability to record lows and highs. The normal human ear generally can hear sounds between 20 Hz and 20,000 Hz, depending upon age, but the typical motion picture projector can only reproduce sounds between 80 Hz and 7,000 Hz. Thus a microphone with a frequency response of less than 80 to 7,000 Hz will provide less than optimum film sound. Conversely, one with a wider frequency response may record sounds the filmmaker's budget will pay for but which the film's audiences will never hear.

The objective during filming is to get the microphone as close as possible to the sound source while keeping it out of camera range. This is usually best accomplished by dangling the microphone from the end of a *boom,* a sturdy pole designed to carry it and its cable, and in some cases to move it in various directions via hand controls at the operator's end.

A mike boom may be attached to a stationary base or tripod, or it may be mounted on a boom dolly, which permits easy, steady movement when necessary during filming. A thinner, lighter version of the mike boom, called a *fishpole,* is held entirely in the hands of the operator.

Occasionally a person whose words are being recorded must move around too actively for a technician to follow with a conventional microphone on a boom. A comparatively economical solution is a *lavaliere,* a special omnidirectional microphone less than half the size of a lipstick, usually worn on a cord around the neck or pinned to clothing.

However, unless it solves some special problem, a lavaliere is generally unsuitable for use in a typical filming session, for a number of reasons. First, its visibility can be a distracting intrusion of the filmmaking process into the picture. And even if artfully concealed, it still can pick up the rustling of clothing. Moreover, its use on the body defeats its omnidirectional capability, limiting its range to the area around the front of the person wearing it.

A better, although more expensive, solution to the problem, as well as for shots in which the sound is too far from the recorder for cables to be practical, is most often found by using a *wireless*

*The fourth basic type of microphone, *bidirectional,* is a familiar sight in radio studios. It records sound directly in front and behind, which is seldom suitable for recording film sound, except for something like an interview.

microphone. This useful unit is also called a *radio microphone,* for it is in fact a tiny radio transmitter, broadcasting on its own FM frequency to a special receiver attached to the recorder. Wireless microphones can be valuable problem-solvers—but one must always be prepared to re-record, which often means re-shoot, in the event that unexpected chatter from a nearby CB radio suddenly becomes an unwelcome addition to the sound track.

Wind blowing against the microphone can be a problem when recording outdoors, but it can also be troublesome on an indoor set every time the microphone is moved, for whether the air is rushing against the mike or the mike is rushing against the air, it is all the same wind noise to the instrument's sensitive diaphragm.

The noise of wind is most often a low-frequency sound, and some microphones are equipped with interior filters which cut out all frequencies below 50 or 100 Hz. However, even when present, these filters are not always reliable, and if wind noise is a serious potential problem for a particular filming session, comparatively inexpensive in-line filters are available which can help substantially.

The most common solution to the problem is the use of a *windscreen,* a specially-designed hood made of acoustical material that slips easily onto the microphone and decreases wind noise. It also can reduce the noises many of us make—with our lips and tongue as well as our breathing—between words when speaking, often unnoticeable to the human ear until they appear on a sound track.

Camera Noise Mufflers While some cameras designed specifically for use in shooting synchronous footage are comparatively quiet, all cameras make *some* noise.* Generally, more expensive cameras are quieter than cheaper cameras.

Before rental or purchase of a used camera, the selected unit should be compared, in operation, with others of the same brand and type, because the more use an individual camera has seen, the noisier it generally becomes.

The muffling of a camera's motor and mechanism noise may be accomplished by use of a specially-designed unit called a *blimp,* a rigid, acoustical housing made to conform to the camera's configuration, and covering it completely.

Despite its somewhat undistinguished name, a blimp can be a

*Camera noise can be a problem even when shooting silent footage, if a filmmaker does not wish the camera to be noticed by the people it is filming.

relatively sophisticated, *and* expensive, piece of equipment. Because it totally encases the camera—including the lens, by means of optically-ground glass—it has special outside controls which can make it unnecessary for the operator to have access to the actual camera controls during filming.

Some cameras are *self-blimped;* others can be fitted with a blimp as an accessory. Since a blimp adds to the size and weight of a camera, its use can decrease the usual mobility of 16mm filming. However, in filming situations that require the maximum possible security against unwanted noise, a blimp is essential.

Somewhat less expensive is a *barney,* which is a padded case or fitted covering available for some cameras. And least expensive of all, but available for *every* camera, is the thick towel some cinematographers carry with them to help reduce the amount of camera noise that reaches the microphone.

THE SOUND OF SILENCE

Often, when the shooting is finished at a professional filming session, everyone is asked to stay quietly in their places as the recorder is turned on, to capture a minute or two of the sound of nothing happening.

What is being taped is called *presence,* and also *room tone* if indoors, consisting of the ambient sound of the locale—breathing, a barely perceptible hum from somewhere far off, the wind blowing in the trees, etc.

As there is no true silence in nature, there is no completely silent moment in a well-produced sound film, for such "dead air" would be clearly noticed by audiences. Accordingly, presence or room tone is used in scenes which were shot silently, or with location dialogue that is postsynchronized in a recording studio, and regularly in the general editing of dialogue and narration tracks.

Presence is especially useful for scenes in which sound has been recorded with a shotgun mike. Such sound can be somewhat unnatural to the ear, because this microphone zeroes in on the target sound with such selectivity that much of the surrounding ambient sound is cut out.

Presence and room tone add a needed depth of realism to dialogue which is dubbed into a scene after filming. It is the lack of proper presence or room tone that makes the dubbed-in dialogue of some foreign films sound so flat and unnatural in the scene.

In editing film sound, the original prerecorded presence of the actual scenes is the most effective, but when it is not available, many studios have general presence tapes, of various environments, for use when needed.

The traditional ritual at the end of filming, which records the living presence of a place, always brings to my mind a line from a poem by Samuel Miller Hageman:

> *"Every sound shall end in silence, but the silence never dies."*

8

THE EDITING OF FILM

It is in the hands of the film editor that all the parts of picture and sound combine. The components originate in many places, such as a set, a location site, a drawing board, a sound studio—but what will later be known as the film itself is actually born in the cutting room.

THE CREATIVE POTENTIAL OF FILM EDITING

Any film is a collection of individual scenes. By their combined merit, they determine the level of quality of the film as a whole. When a scene is particularly good, professionals will say that it "plays." This means that the scene captures and closely holds the viewer's attention; whatever it was meant to do, it *works.*

Whether or not any scene "plays" largely depends on its pacing, which makes the difference between a scene that sits there until replaced by the next one and a scene that *moves,* effortlessly carrying the viewer along with it.

Good pacing is usually the combined result of the scriptwriting, the film editing, *and by the film being shot with the editing in mind.*

The standard professional practice of shooting more film than will actually be used goes to the heart of the shooting-editing relationship, for the very concept of film *editing* implies a number of selections from which a choice can creatively be made.

If a scene were filmed in one continuous shot by a camera fixed at one point, it is possible that it would fulfill its cinematic potential. But "possible" is a word of limited enthusiasm. It is much more likely that the scene would have more dramatic impact, or be more interesting, if presented from different angles, with closeups of faces reacting to what is said, with the camera assuming various focal points of view, and most important, with the rhythm of the scene unerringly built in by the cutting from shot to shot.

Rhythm is a primal force in our lives, harking back to the cave, and we all react to it, sometimes consciously and often quite unknowingly. Whether conveyed in the beat of a drum, or the interworking of the parts of a machine, or the changing shots in a scene, rhythm is not seen or heard so much as it is *felt.* It makes us somehow want to respond—and *that* is exactly what is desired in an audience, by a filmmaker just as much as by a band leader.

TOOLS OF THE CUTTING ROOM

Cutting rooms, like all workplaces, range from Spartan simplicity to opulent splendor, neither of which necessarily reflects upon the skill of the person working there. I have sat on a leopard-skin couch in a panelled room, watching an editor use the latest and most expensive equipment to contribute little to the editing of my film beyond the making of neat splices. And I have teetered on a somewhat unglued wooden chair in a narrow, windowless cubicle, watching as my film, on the most basic rental equipment, was transformed by creative editing into something far better than what had actually been shot.

Film Viewing Equipment Entering the typical cutting room one usually finds the film editor at the editing table. Rolled on its wheels to stand near the table is the *Moviola,* a machine especially designed for the screening of picture and sound work material during the editing process.

Synchronous projection of separate film and track, as on a Moviola, is called *interlock.* (Special interlock projectors, resembling conventional movie projectors, are used for projecting the separate film and sound track of noncomposite films in screening rooms.)

In viewing film on a Moviola, an entire reel can be put on the spindles, or a short length of film may be fed in by hand. On the standard model, the picture is projected onto a small viewing screen,

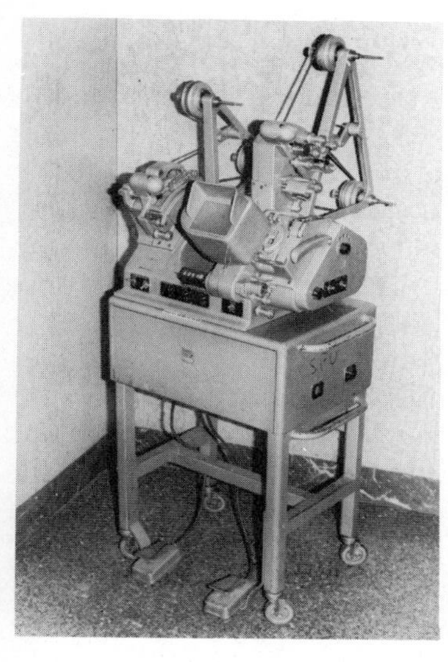

A 35mm Moviola with one sound head. (Photographed at NBC, New York.)

usually about four by five inches, although some models are available with larger screens. Since the lamp in a Moviola does not generate heat as in a conventional film projector, the film can, without burning, be stopped at any frame and kept there for precise selection and marking of a specific point in a scene.

Alongside the viewing unit is the sound unit, powered by a synchronous motor. One or more reels of magnetic track may be put on the spindles, and once their start marks have been positioned under the sound heads, and the film's start mark positioned on the viewing screen, picture and sound remain in perfect synchronization. If desired, picture and sound units can be disengaged, to run either one separately. As with the film, a short length of track may also be fed in by hand.

Each sound unit can read both magnetic and optical tracks, and has an individual volume control. In addition, a master volume control governs the combined sound of all the units, once the operator has adjusted each one satisfactorily.

The small built-in amplifier and speaker of a Moviola provides sound that is utilitarian at best. Although it is adequate for decisions about what sound should go where, editors who want to make more subtle judgments about music often connect the sound heads to a better amplifier and speaker placed nearby. There are connections for a pair of headphones, which could be useful in the case of two editors separately working on adjoining Moviolas.

Film and track can easily be made to go either forward or backward on a Moviola, for study and restudy of a shot or a sound. The speed in either direction may be decreased for slow frame-by-frame examination, or increased to high speed for searching through long reels of footage. If necessary, a hand brake can stop the film and track instantly on a specific frame.

The machine can be operated by an on-off switch, or by separate foot pedals for sound and picture motors when both hands are full of film, marking pencil, script and coffee cup.

The Moviola in the typical cutting room will often be a model with two or three sound units alongside the picture head. Some cutting rooms may also have an "editing Moviola," containing the basic team of picture head plus one sound unit, for use in quickly putting segments of film and track on and off during busy film editing activity.

However, Moviolas equipped with four, five, or even more sound units are frequently used, depending on the requirements, and the budget, of the film project. In addition, extra sound units may be installed on a Moviola which does not have enough of them to serve a film editor's needs.

Moviolas come in various models designed to accommodate different combinations of 16mm and 35mm picture and tracks. This is because 16mm films often use 35mm tracks during editing.

A 35mm Moviola with three sound heads. (Photographed at NBC, New York.)

Thus it is not uncommon to see, for example, a Moviola equipped to play a 16mm picture plus two 35mm tracks and one 16mm track.

An alternative to the upright Moviola, on which the metal reels of film and track are run vertically, is the somewhat more expensive console type of editing machine, sometimes called a *flatbed,* on which film and track are used horizontally in open rolls, wound on cores.

While a Moviola is primarily used only for interlock screening of picture and tracks, with the cutting and splicing being done at a separate editing table, the flatbed permits the editor to accomplish it all while sitting at the console, often with more versatile controls, a bigger viewing screen and quieter operation.

Film Editing Equipment Nearby on the editing table are the two tools which, with the Moviola, form the basic trio of film editing equipment.

A flatbed film editing table, with plates for 16mm film and two 16mm sound tracks. (Courtesy of Arriflex Corp.)

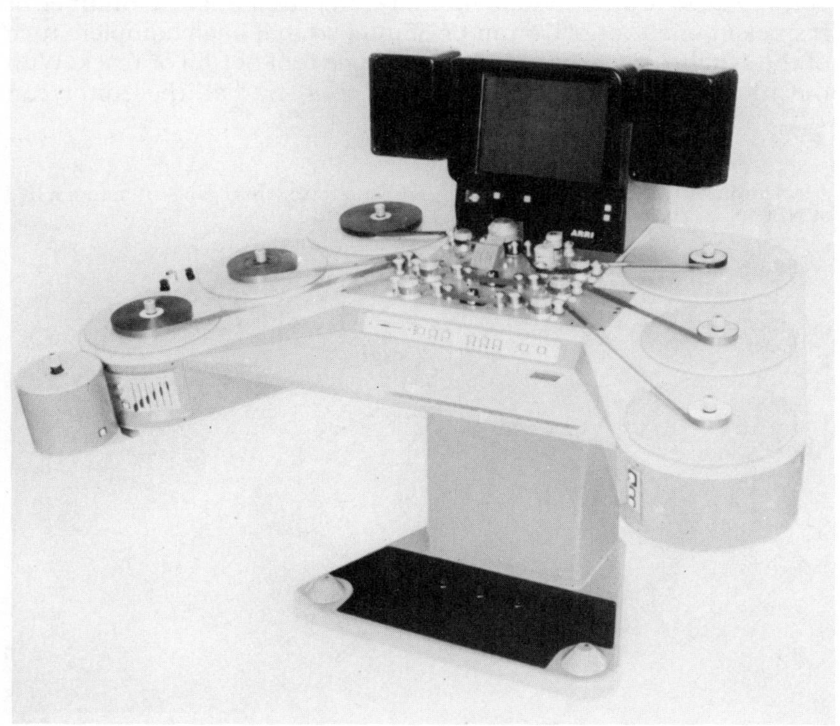

The first, a *synchronizer,* is a device for measuring film and track, and for keeping them in synchronization. As with Moviolas, synchronizers are available in a variety of 16mm/35mm combinations, for working on film of one gauge and tracks of another.

On the synchronizer's shaft are pairs of matching sprocketed wheels, each pair forming a channel, called a *gang,* wide enough to accommodate one of the standard film gauges. Film or track is placed in a channel, where its sprocket holes are engaged, then held in place by a clamp which snaps down over the wheels. The clamp contains two rollers, ensuring smooth movement of the film or track as the editor turns the handle of the shaft, feeding the film or track through the synchronizer either from the left or right.

On the end of the synchronizer is at least one digital footage counter. Some counters measure the film going through the synchronizer in terms of hours, minutes, and seconds instead of footage, but the footage counter is more commonly used (except in television film rooms). Many 16mm/35mm syncronizers have two counters, showing the footage in both gauges.

In addition, mounted on the outside of the first wheel is a *frame counter dial,* a disc containing marks representing the number of frames in one foot of 16mm or 35mm, so that each complete turn of the synchronizer measures exactly one foot of film or track. With the footage counter and the frame counter dial, the editor can

A synchronizer with three 35mm gangs (*left*) and four 16mm gangs. (Photographed at NBC, New York.)

readily measure any length of film or track to the exact frame during editing.

Tape recorder sound heads, especially fitted for use on a synchronizer, are usually installed on some of the gangs and connected to a *tape reader,* a small metal-encased amplifier/speaker, enabling the editor to hear the sound on any tracks as they go through the synchronizer.

Individual gangs can be disengaged to roll freely, allowing the editor to make adjustments in aligning picture in one gang with track in another. Once the editor is satisfied that the film and tracks are synchronized, the gangs are locked.

Thus the precise frame-to-frame alignment possible on the synchronizer gives the editor control of the exact placement of any shot of film in relation to any segment of sound, as narration track is adjusted to picture, as sound effects are inserted, and as the music track is aligned with various scenes.

The most characteristic responsibility of a film editor is, of course, the cutting of film.

A film editor uses one combination tool to cut both film and track and also to join cut pieces together. Although it both cuts and splices, it is simply called a *splicer.* Actually, *they* are called splicers, for there are two types in most cutting rooms: *tape splicers* and *cement splicers.*

Tape splices are made with a strip of specially designed adhesive tape, 16mm or 35mm in width, which is thin and highly transparent for film, and slightly thicker and opaque for magnetic track. The tape has matching sprocket holes which fit over those on the film or track.

The tape splicer contains a platform on which the film is positioned, by sprockets, so that the selected frame line is directly under the blade. A tamper, on a spring, is brought down to tamp the film securely onto the sprockets, and then a hinged blade, also on a spring, comes down to make the cut.

The piece of cut film with the unwanted scene is then removed, and a length of film containing a new scene replaces it on the platform, to be spliced to the film waiting there.

Magnetic track is cut and spliced much the same way.

A tape splice can be made quickly and undone easily, but it can be quite visible on the screen. Even if an editor carefully positions the tape to end at a frame line, instead of in the middle of a frame, the film is thrown slightly out of focus each time a tape splice goes through the projector. Therefore, tape splices are primarily meant to be temporary, such as the splices on a work print which may be

A 16mm tape splicer. (Photographed at NBC, New York.)

opened and closed many times as shots are changed around during editing and re-editing.

Unlike a tape splice, in which two ends of film are butted together, the ends of film in a cement splice slightly overlap each other. In 16mm film, which has less room between frames than the larger 35mm film, this overlap extends into the picture area, which means that one frame of picture is "lost" in a 16mm work print each time a cement splice is made. Editors therefore will often insert a one-frame slug of *leader* (the blank film ordinarily spliced to the beginning of a reel for threading on a projector or Moviola) at each cement splice in a 16mm work print, to maintain exact synchronization with tracks during editing. The frame loss is remedied when the negative is cut and assembled (as discussed later).

A 35/16mm cement splicer. (Photographed at NBC, New York.)

Before a cement splice is made, the emulsion (the shiny top portion containing the picture) is removed from the piece of film that overlaps, by a special built-in scraper. This is to expose the base of the film, so that the film cement (which is actually a strong solvent) can dissolve the base of one film into the base of the other, literally fusing them together. The twin top portions of the splicer then come down and are locked against the bottom platform, tightly pressing the cemented film between them.

Most cement splicers contain a small heating element, since the splice is more secure if it is warmed during the bond. Consequently, a cement splicer is more often called a "hot splicer."

Cement splices are made only on film; magnetic track is always spliced with tape.

Since a cement splice is actually more of a weld than a splice, it is much more secure. In addition, it is much less visible when projected. For both these reasons, cement splices are almost always used in the splicing of negatives and release prints.

The synchronizer and splicer are used on the editing table, in the center of which is a built-in *light box,* comprised of a sheet of light-diffusing glass, mounted flush with the table's surface and thick enough to bear the weight of the synchronizer, splicer, or other editing tools. Lit from below by a bulb, the light box back-lights any frames of film the editor wants to examine.

Among the items usually found in the drawer of a typical editing table are some pairs of white cotton *film gloves,* always worn when handling negative material; a bottle of film cleaner; a magnifying glass, for closely studying individual frames of film without putting them on the Moviola; and some cloth wipes or a piece of clean velvet, to run a completed film through, for removal of dust.

Mounted on each side of the table is a *rewind,* a long spindle attached to a hand crank, upon which one or more reels of film or track can be placed, to be wound onto empty reels on the other rewind, or as a resting place for the reels of film while being edited.

Labs and other film processors handling large volumes of film have electrically-powered, high-speed rewinds, but most film editors use manual models, for they are usually not interested in moving film quickly from rewind to rewind, but rather in doing something to it as it hangs between them.

Within easy reach is at least one *film bin,* a large free-standing metal container which usually has a protective cloth lining, to hold clips of film currently being used in editing. The film, which can range from single frames to lengths of a hundred feet or more, is hung in various groupings on the pins of a rack mounted over the bin. Although both rectangular and round shapes are commonly used, all film bins are familiarly called "film barrels."

The reels of film that accumulate in an active cutting room are kept on special racks along the wall, whose shelves are designed to hold the weight of many thousands of feet of film, since a thousand feet in 35mm represents only about eleven minutes of footage.

In addition to the basic film editing equipment, two accessories are often found in a well-equipped cutting room.

One is a *sound reader.* Having no transport motor, a sound reader is usually put on the editing table between the rewinds, and a reel of track is fed through it. Some sound readers will read not only magnetic tracks, but also the optical sound track on composite films. Sound readers are available in 16mm, 35mm, and 16mm/35mm combination models.

A typical cutting room. The film editor (*right*), running the Moviola by way of the foot pedal, discusses the editing of a scene with the film's producer (*the author*). Behind them is a film bin and film racks. (Photo by Michael Becker at Custom Films/Video, Inc., Westport, Connecticut.)

Specific sounds on a track can be found more readily with a sound reader than with a Moviola, for the track may be moved back and forth to isolate the sound very easily on a sound reader, while a Moviola requires repeated switching of the motor from forward to reverse. Sound readers are especially useful in searching for particular sound segments on long reels of track, since the track may be fed through the reader as fast as the operator can crank the rewinds.

Another useful accessory is a *viewer,* for either 16mm or 35mm, and available in silent or sound models. A viewer is the visual equivalent of the sound reader in that it is particularly useful for isolating a specific camera shot for close study and for searching through long reels of material quickly.

THE CRAFT OF THE FILM EDITOR

Film editors are often busy in the producer's behalf far beyond the cutting room. They are frequently at or in contact with the optical house, the lab, the sound studio, the graphic artist, and other suppliers of creative and technical services. But it is the building of the film-to-be, shot by shot and scene by scene on the cutting table, that makes the film editor's work so central to the production of a film.

This is illustrated by the fact that the film editor did not wait for this chapter in which to make an appearance. Instead, almost all the aspects of production discussed in the previous pages cited some relationship to the editing of the film. In fact, one sees a montage of film editors going about their typical work from these references to the cutting room in various earlier chapters:

Examining clips of film in the barrel for a shot to cover a particular narration line. . . . Choosing the reaction shot that works best in a scene. . . . Conferring with the producer about the design of a special effect. . . . Building an exchange of dialogue between two people whose lines were actually filmed separately on different days. . . . Carefully selecting the placement of an establishing shot in a sequence so that it appears naturally. . . . Deleting fifteen seconds from the middle of a two-minute shot of a person talking continuously, by inserting a cutaway shot. . . . Bringing film into synchronization by marking the frame in which clapsticks first come together. . . . Cutting into the master shot of a scene to insert POV shots and other angles, to highlight and punctuate the dialogue and action.

As the editor goes about characteristic activities like these, and others, the focus of all efforts is the work print.

Editing the Work Print What a first draft is to text, a work print is to film.

As the editor receives each segment of film or sound, sometimes together in sync and sometimes separately, they are edited and then inserted into the work print and its accompanying track. They are not necessarily inserted consecutively, since picture and sound elements are not always shot, recorded, or otherwise obtained in the same order in which they will appear in a film.

Thus a typical work print might have a few scenes in a row . . . then some blank leader, aligned with a recorded narration on the accompanying track, to mark the place of some awaited scene . . . then a few more scenes, lined up with the appropriate narration . . . then possibly some more leader, where graphics are scheduled to appear . . . then a scene aligned with its synchronous sound on the track . . . then a silent scene, etc.

Every segment of film that comes into the editor's hand, to be edited and then put into the work print, is a print that has been made especially for editing purposes; its negative, like the negative of all material for the film project, remains untouched in its original form.

Ultimately, when the editor has cut and recut the work print into its final version, those negatives will be the basis for ultimately translating the work print into the release prints that audiences will see.

The key to matching the shots in the work print, no matter how much the editor has cut and trimmed and rearranged them, to the same shots in the original negatives, is the use of *edge numbers.*

Film manufacturers put a series of numbers along the edge of original motion picture film. When the film is processed at the lab after a filming session, the edge numbers print through from each negative onto the print made from it, linking each shot in the print to the matching shot in the negative.

Because edge numbers are much easier to read in 35mm than in 16mm, many filmmakers routinely have new, clearly legible, matching edge numbers put on all of their 16mm negatives and prints after filming. However, film editors often have matching edge numbers put on 35mm material as well, such as when ordering a duplicate negative plus matching duplicate print of some work material. These specially-ordered edge numbers, printed on by a lab, are usually called *code numbers,* to differentiate them in the cutting room and lab from the edge numbers that appear on new film.

A film editor spends much of his or her time in the cutting room working as a sound editor as well.

For example, after a narration has been recorded wild, and the sound studio has transferred the sound on the quarter-inch tape to 16mm or 35mm magnetic sound film, the editor adjusts picture and sound to each other—trimming the track by reducing the space between words or deleting breaths, extending or shortening shots and scenes in the film—until picture and narration are in a harmony that appears perfectly natural.

In addition, besides inserting sound effects throughout the film, the editor aligns the various parts of the music track with different scenes, pulling it up here, moving it down there, until it works effectively wherever it is heard.

Each track is usually on a separate roll, and each roll is made to be exactly the same length as the work print by inserting blank leader or scrap film between the places where the sound actually is heard. Thus, once the reels are lined up together at their start marks, the sound on each reel will be in the right place in relation to the picture.

Besides the transfer of quarter-inch recording tape, other kinds of sound transfers are made regularly during everyday film production. For example, a producer may want to use some scenes from the composite print of some other, completed film, and the sound from the desired scenes will be transferred from the film's built-in optical sound track to 16mm or 35mm magnetic sound film. (In addition, a silent color or black-and-white duplicate print will be made from the other film's negative, so that the film editor has the usual work print plus separate track for use in editing the borrowed scenes.)

Scene Transitions As a work print evolves toward its completion in the cutting room, film editors address one of the most basic creative responsibilities in the making of a film: deciding (often subject to the producer's or director's approval) how the various scenes shall come in and go out. They do this, when preparing the completed work print for optical effects, by marking each point where one scene ends and another begins with standard symbols indicating which transitional device the optical house should use.

There are four basic scene transitions:

Cuts. Cutting is the most common method of changing scenes in any film. The editor selects what is to be the last frame of film in Scene A, and then simply splices it to what has been chosen as the first frame of film in Scene B, resulting in an instantaneous change from one to the other. While the effect of this on the screen can be barely noticeable, it more often is crisp, or even abrupt, depending upon the content of the two scenes at that point.

Dissolves. Softer transitions between scenes are accomplished by using dissolves. Although there is an illusion that one scene is "dissolving" into the other, what actually happens on the screen is a deliberate double exposure, as the incoming and outgoing scenes simply overlap for a few moments. The number of frames from each scene which overlap is what determines the length, and thereby the dramatic effect, of the dissolve. Some usual lengths are eight overlapping frames (one-third of a second) for a short dissolve, forty-eight frames (two seconds) for a medium dissolve, and seventy-two frames (three seconds) when a more lingering effect is desired.

Fades. Fading out and fading in represent more of a break in continuity between scenes, something like the effect of a curtain rising or falling on a scene in the theatre. Technically, a fade is the same as a dissolve, except that the faded scene overlaps some frames of solid black or white leader.

Wipes. In a wipe, the incoming scene moves into the frame by "wiping away" the current scene until it completely replaces it on the screen. Although the typical wipe moves from left to right or right to left, the incoming scene can start to replace the existing scene from any point on the screen, moving in from the top, the bottom, or diagonally from a corner. In the frequently-used *flipover wipe* (more commonly called a *flip*), the existing scene seems to abruptly flip over on the screen to reveal the incoming scene on its reverse side. In another wipe, the new scene begins to appear in checkerboard fragments which expand to fill the screen.*

The more standard left-to-right and right-to-left wipes, which abounded in the movies of the thirties and early forties (especially Westerns), were often used primarily to indicate that the new scene was happening simultaneously—a kind of cinematic "Meanwhile . . . " Today they can fulfill that same purpose, but are more frequently selected simply as interesting transitions that work better than a cut or a dissolve between two particular scenes.

While cuts, dissolves, fades and wipes may be considered the four basic scene transitions, the *swish pan* is also regularly used, although (as discussed earlier in Chapter 6) it is appropriate only in certain circumstances.

Some scene transitions can be accomplished by a lab during the printing stage, instead of by an optical house, at a saving in cost. In preparation for this, the editor must separate the entire film into at least two rolls, the odd-numbered scenes in one roll and the even-numbered scenes in the other, with each roll containing slugs of blank leader between the scenes. The slugs in the first roll correspond to the lengths of the scenes in the second roll, and vice versa. This procedure, called *A & B roll* or *checkerboard* editing and printing, permits basic effects, such as cuts, fades, dissolves, and some titles, to be put on a film during the printing process. However, few of the more interesting visual devices an optical printer can provide for scene changing, such as flips or other wipes, are possible with this method.

Rough Cut to Fine Cut A work print starts out, and during much of the editing remains, a *rough cut:* the basic content is there, but many of the scenes run long, and some scenes not yet available on film are

*How this and other optical effects are accomplished is discussed later in this chapter, in *Film Opticals.*

represented by blank leader. Eventually it will become a *fine cut,* a work print that is at, or very near, what the editor considers completion.

In building a rough cut into a fine cut, the craft of film editing is performed on three levels.

The first is the editing of the film as a total work. The editor keeps this perspective in mind as the editing progresses from the first cut to the final screening.

Second, using the various shots provided for the purpose, each individual scene is carefully constructed, both as a link in a chain of scenes that forms the total film, and as an individual entity with substance and meaning of its own.

But at the heart of it all is the basic unit of film—the shot. It is the editing of the shots that lays the foundation for the editing of the film as a whole, and illustrates why the *cutting* of film is the creative basis for the craft.

In a well-edited film, each individual camera shot is truly edited—which entails more than careful selection by the editor, or by the producer or director at the editor's side.

Key considerations are the beginning and end of each shot, for they are its entrance and exit points in the scene.

Then, every shot contains a portion which represents the essence of whatever it is that caused it to be filmed—something it shows, something it says, something that contrasts it with a previous shot. In trimming the shot for use in the scene, the editing blade must cut into it at precisely the right point to best show this essence within the required length.

Finally, not ending a shot a few frames too soon—for example, just before a person's hand comes down *completely* to his or her side—reflects a sensitivity to the movement in a scene that is one of the essentials of good editing.*

FILM GRAPHICS

Almost all films contain titles, and many of them, especially nontheatrical films, contain other graphic elements as well.

These, like everything else in the film, must be represented in the editor's work print, either by being put on film and inserted, or by

*These judgments cannot really be made without running the film at true sound speed. That is why, unlike an amateur, a professional film editor must have a machine like the Moviola.

an indication on the work print of the places in which they will eventually appear in the completed film.

Artwork and Titles Film graphics require a special kind of creativity, as well as an appreciation of the difference between the function of graphics for film and for printed media. Therefore, any corporate art department primarily geared to create other kinds of graphics may, or may not, be suitable for a film producer's needs.

Professional art and graphics studios are a more certain source of artwork and titles for films. A professional graphics house not only can fulfill the creative requirements for film graphics, but they are usually equipped to follow through by providing the elements—whether artwork to be drawn or painted, or words to be set in type—in the right form and on the right materials to be shot on film, as required.

Animation Sometimes animation can fill a visual need to replace what is unavailable, or even nonexistent. It can make numbers and percentages often more meaningful, and always more palatable.

In any film, animation can be used alone, or it can be integrated into the live action, which is a more complex process.

There are two general types of animation: *cartoon,* in which drawn figures are made to move; and *technical* or *graphic animation,* in which numbers, graphs, and diagrams come alive on the screen. Technical animation has transformed many classroom lessons from educational ordeals into delights of learning, and this successful technique has been adapted into an equally effective sales tool in the business world.

More than most other types of film, animation relies on music and sound effects for its optimal success, for although it can be silently entertaining and communicative, its synchronization with music beats and other sounds gives animation its greatest impact.

Sometimes the sound for animation is postsynchronous, recorded to fit existing animation drawings. More often, sound tracks are recorded wild before the animation house starts its work, and are brought to the film editor, who analyzes them.

This involves carefully listening to each track and notating where each syllable of every word appears, both in a written log of footage and frame counts, and by writing each syllable, wherever it is heard, directly on the track itself. The same precise notation is made for music beats.

The film editor turns the analyzed tracks over to the animation house, where they are used to prepare a *bar sheet,* which provides the animator with an exact frame-by-frame guide for the length of each individual animated movement.

The principle of animation is still basically the shooting of dozens or even hundreds of individual photographs, each only slightly different, which give the illusion of motion when projected consecutively.

But while the principle is basically the same, the practice has become increasingly complex, as technology replaces tedium in much of the process today. Many busy animation houses use sophisticated computerized systems to accomplish the age-old trick of "making the stick figures move."

An animated sequence, when completed, generally arrives from the animation house as one continuous segment in exactly the prearranged length, with all scene transitions, such as fades and dissolves, built into it. Thus a film editor usually has little or no editing to do to it and merely inserts the segment, and the track to which it is synchronized, into the appropriate place in the work print.

When appropriate, animation is an extremely useful and versatile tool of film production, for it enables filmmakers not only

A computerized animation stand. The camera (*A*) with interchangeable 16mm/36mm lenses is aimed downward on its vertical carriage above the stand. The operator is using a teleprinter to program the desired moves onto punch tape, and can also control the animation filming by way of a computer terminal (*B*). (Photo by Susan A. Berg at I.F. Studios, Inc., New York.)

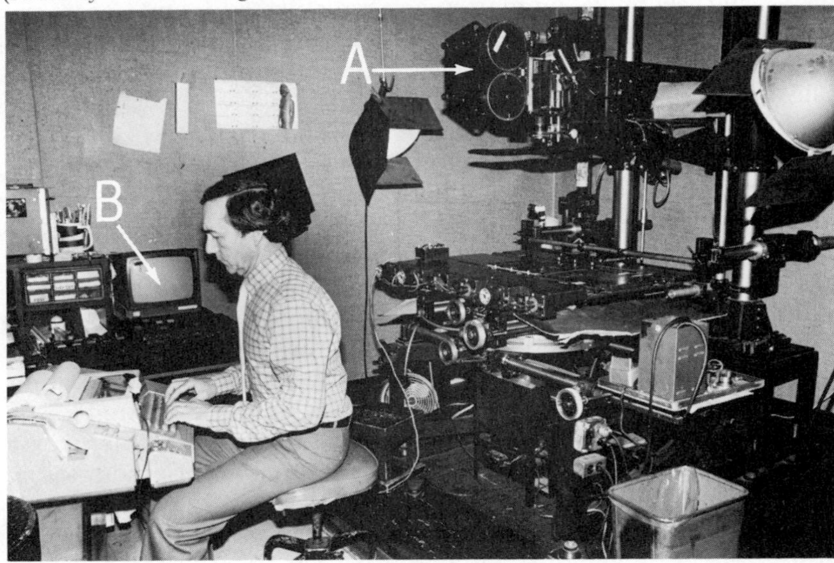

to control reality, but to go a step further and create a unique new reality of their own.

FILM OPTICALS

If there is any one line between amateur and professional filmmaking, it is at the door of the optical house.

Most of the high technical quality and much of the creativity of today's theatrical and nontheatrical films are the result of optical effects.

While film audiences are generally aware of film opticals in the form of *special effects,* from the antics of an invisible dog to the on-screen collision of two fully populated planets, they seldom really notice the more familiar optical effects such as the fades and dissolves which change each scene.

A typical optical house contains an array of highly specialized equipment, but the heart of it all is the *optical printer,* which combines the functions of camera and projector, in a series of

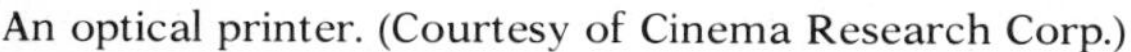

An optical printer. (Courtesy of Cinema Research Corp.)

re-photographing steps which add new picture material or change existing picture material.

It can shoot a selected portion of each frame of picture in a scene; then, by the use of *mattes,* which are photographic masks made in specific shapes as needed, it can insert those portions into the frames of picture of another scene. This is how wipes are accomplished, as well as how a film can show a person apparently only six inches tall seemingly standing in the palm of a normally sized person's hand.

With few exceptions, whatever a filmmaker may envision happening on the screen, an optical house can make possible (although film budgets have a way of underlining the fine distinction between "possible" and "feasible"). On a regular basis, however, an optical house is more frequently used to serve three regular needs of everyday film production.

First, the optical printer makes the standard cuts, dissolves, fades, wipes, and flips most often used as transitions between scenes. Many other transitional devices are possible, including special wipes in made-to-order shapes.

Another familiar requirement of everyday film production, the blowing up of 16mm film and the reduction of 35mm, is regularly done at the optical house.

Finally, titles and captions are usually put on a film by the optical printer, with the choice of either *fade on . . . fade off* or the crisper *pop on . . . pop off* titling.

Besides these standard services, the optical printer makes technically possible, and readily available, many of the creative touches that can enhance a film. These might include manipulating the actual speed of action in a scene; splitting the screen into two or more parts, with separate scenes running in each; superimposing a face from one scene onto the action in another scene; or abruptly suspending action altogether, by consecutively printing the same frame of film for a *freeze frame* effect.

In departing from the optical effects commonly used in everyday film production, theoretically *anything* can be accomplished on the screen. Nevertheless, I feel that an optical effect, like any other technical wonder available to the filmmaker, should always be a medium of creativity—not a substitute for it.

I could not end this chapter without noting that, although it is seldom acknowledged, film editors have always been a great unsung corps of teachers in the film industry. Countless producers owe the foundation of what they know about film production to what they originally learned from the film editors they ostensibly were supervising.

9
MUSIC ON FILM

Music is a primal force. Its basic role in our lives, and its untapped potential, are only now starting to be truly understood. And nowhere is it a more potent factor than in film production.

Music has been an integral part of filmmaking from the earliest moving pictures—for the "silents" were only silent in their production, not in their presentation, which was usually accompanied by appropriate music from each movie house's piano player.

A music score's true impact on a film is seldom fully appreciated by its viewers, since they do not have the opportunity of observing the "before and after" effect, which can be most impressive to those involved in the production.

MUSIC AS A CREATIVE TOOL

Music's primary contribution to a film is its invaluable ability to evoke a mood, to provide a desired atmosphere. However, a good film score can serve four other functions which are often just as important, if not as apparent.

1. *Music can provide effective punctuation to specific action.* There is an incomparable effect when an action, or a series of movements, happens on screen to the accompaniment of musical chords or beats or stings which "hit" exactly in time. What, unscored, was only noticeable now becomes interesting or even exciting, because it invokes the innate human response to rhythm.
2. *Music can convey a sense of continuity,* more clearly linking a series of associated scenes which, because of their content, might otherwise seem less related.
3. *Music can emphasize a definite transition or change* from one scene or sequence to another, when needed.
4. *Music can enhance or even establish the setting,* imparting a sense of location which may be lacking pictorially. For example, a shot of a rural area (perhaps actually in Vermont) becomes "Western open spaces" when music with an appropriate Western flavor identifies it as such to an audience.

An important consideration in the use of film music is its placement in relation to the spoken word, whether dialogue or narration.

Every piece of music has a "voice," derived from a combination of its melody, its harmonic structure and its rhythm. Depending on the music, this voice may be unobtrusive or it may be clear and quite articulate. The objective is to keep what the score is expressing musically from conflicting with what is being expressed verbally. On a well-balanced track, the music can be eloquent when it is heard alone—but when words are being spoken, the music should either reinforce their message or be the unobtrusive sonic "carpet" it is often called in the sound studio.

SOURCES OF FILM MUSIC

Professional films are primarily scored in one of two ways—by an original score, which is composed and recorded especially for the film, or by prerecorded music provided by a commercial music library.

Theatrical motion pictures, of course, usually have original scores, sometimes more popular than the films for which they were written. Major television documentary series often feature specially-written background music, the most notable of which was Richard Rodgers' memorable score for the "Victory At Sea" series. Most television commercials for major brand products have original scores, usually composed by specialists in that field.

Most other film production relies on commercial music libraries as the source of material for film scores, including individual television documentaries, television commercials with average-sized budgets—and the bulk of all professional nontheatrical films.

The principal reason is that an original score—which involves a composer's fee, arranger's and copyist's fees, the cost of musicians, recording studio rental, etc., plus subsequent editing—costs substantially more than the average commercial library charge.

Theoretically, an original score is preferable, just as a tailor-made suit theoretically is better than one off the rack. However, just as there are some excellent suits to be found on the racks, commercial music libraries can be excellent sources of music for a film.

"Music houses," as they are more familiarly known, are found in many larger cities and contain tapes and disks of hundreds of musical selections which were recorded, primarily in Europe, specifically for use as background music.

Their lengths vary from two-second "stings"—to either foretell or punctuate suspense, drama, terror, triumph, etc.—to works of ten minutes or more. The musical selections most auditioned by the typical film producer at a music house are from thirty seconds to three minutes.

The titles of the musical segments are often vividly descriptive, which is extremely useful in the auditioning and selection process. Thus, for a scene showing a woman afraid of some figures lurking in the shadows of a deserted street, you know that a 30-second segment called "Night Fear" is worth auditioning.

The evocative titles also help to recall music segments which work particularly well, thereby sometimes avoiding the need to audition and select music when time is precious. For example, needing music to score a scene involving an ominous building-up of tension, I clearly remembered "Maniac Pursuit," which I had used quite successfully more than eleven years earlier; after getting it with only a telephone call, it worked just as well again.

A typical use of a commercial music library would involve a film producer making an appointment, coming in, and describing the film or showing a few of its scenes on the music house's screening equipment, and specifying the kind of music he or she is seeking for the film as a whole, or for certain segments.

Frequently a producer will be accompanied by a film editor, for although the producer usually knows what kind of music is wanted in general terms, such as the mood and tempo, the film editor usually has a more precise idea of how the music must work at certain specific points in particular scenes.

After auditioning various musical candidates, the producer

makes a selection, often based on advice of the music house staff, and the music is transferred from the library's master disk or quarter-inch tape to 16mm or 35mm magnetic sound film, for use by the film editor.

The selected music may be edited to film by the music house, in which case a work print is turned over to them and one of their staff music editors custom tailors the score to the film. This is because, while the average film editor can and regularly does edit the music for any film he or she is working on, sometimes the music is considered to be such an important factor that the services of a specialist are desired.

For example, some fast-moving action in a comedic scene may really only be as funny as it seems because of the music to which it is synchronized. Or, in a documentary, the impact of a series of camera shots may rely on the rhythmic music to which the shots change. Or a producer simply may feel that the contribution the overall musical score makes to each scene is particularly important to the film's success.

The cost of library music, without editing, usually depends on how the film containing the music is used—a one-time-only showing, three scheduled showings, unlimited multiple use within a certain time period, etc.

For films I have produced, I have used commercial library music and I have commissioned original scores, and while I have been satisfied by both methods, I feel that library music often offers a filmmaker a greater measure of production control. When you are discussing a prospective film score with a composer, you can explain what you want and expect, as fully and clearly as possible. And the composer can demonstrate that he or she understands completely, and is willing to provide it. However, you never really know what the score will be like, in its finished form, until you hear it for the first time at a rehearsal, played by musicians you have already contracted, in a recording studio you have already rented.

At a good music house, however, you can audition countless selections until you find the very piece, or combination of pieces, you want—and when you leave, you *know* what you have.

An interesting and growing source of film music, straddling the areas of both original scoring and library music, is *synthesized music,* which is produced by means of electronics instead of with the conventional catgut, reeds, or strings.

Synthesized music no longer is confined to what may be played on a musico-electronic instrument, such as the Moog Synthesizer; the sound of any musical instrument can now be recreated with uncanny realism by sophisticated devices incorporating digital computers.

One advantage to synthesized music is that it not only can sound either conventionally musical or "electronic," but offers the creative possibilities of combining the two in any musical segment.

Synthesized music is finding increasing use as part of, and as an enhancement to, the prerecorded stock at music libraries, especially for the scoring of television commercials.

EDITING MUSIC FOR FILM

A skilled professional music editor can delete phrases, switch passages around, combine parts of different movements into one, edit chords or even individual notes—completely transforming a piece of music beyond the familiar limits of what can be written by a composer and played by musicians on their instruments.

There are, however, some relatively simpler aspects of music editing which can be accomplished personally by a filmmaker, by altering the original speed or direction of music. As the following examples show, this can be done with segments of music that may have been shortened to a desired length but otherwise are used intact.

Reverse Music Playing any recorded musical note backwards—on a playback machine that is running in reverse—produces an unusual effect.

Although few of us are actually aware of it, we are accustomed to the reverberation that follows the playing of a note. Depending on the instrument, this may be faintly but clearly evident, such as when a piano note is struck, or it may be almost imperceptible, and thus felt as much as heard. When recorded music is played backwards, this sequence is reversed: *we hear the reverberation first, and then the note.* The effect of this on listeners is subtle but interesting, and not readily identifiable by them.

When notes are heard collectively in a passage, the effect is even more interesting. We hear the familiar sequence of note . . . reverberation . . . note . . . reverberation, etc.—but while the sequence is familiar, the sound somehow is not. This is because the usual sequence is *note C . . . note C's reverberation . . . note D . . . note D's reverberation, etc.* But now, instead, it is *note D . . . note C's reverberation . . . note C . . . note B's reverberation, etc.* The harmonic effect is impossible for musicians to duplicate on their instruments, and is therefore markedly different from what we are accustomed to hearing.

Variable Speed Music Music normally played at a fast tempo conveys a familiar sense of elation or excitement. But when music that was not originally written to be played fast *is* played that way, by increasing the speed of the playback machine, the resultant artificial rise in pitch gives the music an arresting "edge" that can be most expressive.

Conversely, when music is played back more slowly than it was actually recorded, the result is an unmistakable lowering of mood setting.

In both cases, the effectiveness of the technique depends on the selection of the music to be sped up or slowed down; but also in both cases, the degree is controllable, according to whatever effect is desired for a particular shot, scene, or sequence.

Using Music "As Is" Even more simple, and therefore easier to do without the services of a music editor, is selecting a piece of music and using it, exactly as it is, to score something short, from a ten-second television spot to a five-minute film. This technique has the virtue of not only being easy but also fast, which is sometimes a more important consideration.

Barring coincidence, the selected piece of music is seldom exactly the length of the picture it is meant to score. Let us say the music segment is four minutes, and the film it is meant to accompany runs only three minutes. This means a decision must be made about which portion of the four minutes of music to use: the first three minutes, the last three minutes, or a three-minute section in the middle.

This decision might be influenced by a distinctive musical phrase or beat in one part of the music, but a selected short piece of music is often uniform in melody and tempo throughout, except for some kind of ending. Therefore, the most satisfactory choice is usually to "tail-sync" the music—to align it with the picture so that the last chord, or beat, coincides with the last action in the film.

For example, if our four-minute piece of music—selected for use behind three minutes of film—were started anywhere but exactly three minutes before its final note, it would have to go out (when the film ended) either in an artificial musical fade, which might not be appropriate to the music at that point, or in an unceremonious "dump"—meaning the music abruptly cuts out, wherever it happens to be musically. A dump may chance to fall at a convenient musical point, but more often a few incoming notes from the next musical phrase are awkwardly left hanging.

However, even a fade-out done as unobtrusively as possible is not as desirable as a true natural ending to a piece of music. A film's audience is not likely to remember whether some music faded in or started naturally—but they certainly will notice how it ends.

In the case of shorter films, aligning music with picture so that a distinctive final chord or beat exactly coincides with the last action on screen provides what is called a musical "button," which can be an extremely effective audiovisual exclamation point to the film as a whole.

Music is a beautiful element, even when you are only passively enjoying it; but when you use its sonic brush strokes to fill in and enliven the background of moving pictures, you appreciate even more what a wondrous thing it is.

10 SOUND EFFECTS ON FILM

In film production, the phrase MUSIC & EFX is a familiar one on the labels of cans and boxes, and it is appropriate that music and sound effects are usually categorized together, for sound effects represent the true background music of everyday life.

SOUND AS A CREATIVE TOOL

There are six primary uses of sound effects in a typical film, some creative, some practical, and others a combination of both.

To add what is not there, but should be. This is perhaps the basic use of sound effects in a film. There are many reasons why the appropriate sound may not actually accompany an action during filming.

For one, in traditional Hollywood movie-making the sound that really matters to the technicians handling the microphones and controlling the recording equipment is the dialogue. The rest of the sounds may be dubbed in later.

Sometimes this is because the incidental sounds actually being made at the time—the closing of a door, the clinking of glassware, etc.—are not precisely what the filmmaker wants them to be.

And sometimes it is simply because the normal sound does not exist during filming. For example, except for one or two close insert shots, there usually is no real baby in the bundle being cradled so lovingly in the arms of the actress or actor on the screen. This is partly because of the laws limiting the use of infants in movie-making; but in addition, since babies seldom perform according to any script but their own, even when they are actually before the cameras their cries, gurgles and coos are best dubbed in later as sound effects.

To evoke a mood. The howl of a wolf, or the sound of the wind sweeping across the empty moors, often can infuse a scene with an atmosphere more effectively than any music.

To do this, the filmmaker often creatively uses the *volume* of familiar, ordinary sounds, applying not the usual volume, but one that fulfills some dramatic purpose.

This might be in a scene of a frightened person lying in bed in a dark room late at night, suddenly hearing the sound of the lock surreptitiously being tried, and perhaps finally clicking open. Or a scene in which a woman is in a bedroom, her lover having just stormed out in anger; hoping he will return from the next room, she hears instead the sound of the apartment door shutting with an expressive slam.

To make a statement, or convey an impression. A filmmaker may select one of the sounds, rather than any of the dialogue or action, to communicate the principal point of a scene. For example, the slow, steady creak of an old person's rocking chair can convey a sense of time going by in tedium.

Occasionally a sound used for this purpose is one that the audience understands is not supposed to exist literally in the scene, sometimes known as *expressionistic sound.* A vivid example of this might be, during a dinner party, the pounding of a jackhammer heard over a close shot of the face of someone with a headache.

To expand the physical dimensions of a scene. Envision the interior of a film studio. In one corner a set has been prepared, depicting a campsite in the woods. From the prop tree on the left border to the artificial bush on the right, the set is approximately fifteen feet wide. The studio is dark, and the set has been artfully lit for nighttime. Two actors dressed in outdoor clothes sit on either side of a crackling campfire. Occasionally the leaves on some nearby trees are gently moved by the wind of an unseen studio blower.

All in all, the scene, as viewed in the camera, is most realistic. However, the campsite is still only fifteen feet wide. The set decorator cannot really do anything about that—but a sound engineer *can,* with the right sound effects.

The rush of a stream or the muffled roar of a waterfall heard as though coming from a half mile away, plus the faroff cry of a train whistle now and then, can believably enlarge the scope of the surrounding woods far beyond what is actually framed by the camera lens.

To depict something that is happening off-screen. Occasionally it is necessary for something to happen in a screen story which, it is decided, should not actually be shown on screen.

It may be a simple question of taste, because the action is considered too gruesome.

Or it may be a matter of creative judgment, whereby it is thought that, as on radio, the event would be much more dramatic to the audience if seen in their "theatre of the mind."

Or perhaps it is decided that the dramatic focus is so clearly on someone reacting to what happens that the event itself might distract from the impact of that reaction.

Thus sound effects can sometimes be a key factor in conveying an important *visual* message on the screen.

To mask or lessen some other sound. Sometimes an unwanted sound cannot be deleted from the sound track. It may be the result of a technical problem, such as the noise of a generator during filming. Or it may simply be bad luck on location, such as some unknown person yelling "Here, Rover!" quite unexpectedly from nearby, recorded on the last few inches of tape available during synchronous filming.

And it is not unknown for a director to yell "Cut!" too soon, stepping on the last word of filmed dialogue or narration.

An unwanted sound can usually be removed by a skillful editor, no matter how close it is to adjacent spoken words. But if it is *behind* a word on the track, it generally cannot be deleted effectively.

Sometimes it is possible to have the same voice record the word(s) for insertion, or else try to lessen the problem with music. But more often it requires masking with a sound effect, carefully selected so that it not only covers the unwanted sound but also seems appropriate in that place on the track.

The application of sound effects can be a more extensive undertaking than working with music. This is because the average scene usually can be scored with only one segment of music, but often requires a number of different sound effects, which must not only sound right individually, but also in relation to other sounds in the scene.

In combining various sound effects, some blend well with speech and with other sounds, and some do not. For example, a sharper, relatively high-pitched sound, such as an auto horn, would clearly emerge from a group of sounds, and could conflict with dialogue or narration if used behind it. However, lower-pitched, less assertive sounds, such as a well-tuned car motor, are more sonically sociable, in that they mix well with, and do not tend to fight, other sounds and spoken words.

SOURCES OF FILM SOUND EFFECTS

Just as there are commercial music libraries, there are commercial sound effects libraries in many larger cities, although generally fewer in number than the music houses. Many of them will provide catalogues, describing the sounds they have on hand, including their lengths and prices.

In addition, most music libraries also supply sound effects; some music houses, in fact, specialize in both areas.

At a commercial library, a sound effect can take longer to select than music, which could make it more expensive in search time. This is because clients frequently have only a general idea of what the "right" piece of music would sound like, and thus may be quickly satisfied by one of the likely candidates brought out by the librarian. However, they usually know exactly what a particular sound is like, and until they hear what they recognize as precisely the *boink* made by a multi-flanged eyelet grinder in single-action operation, the librarian has to keep searching.

Most professional sound recording studios have a number of the most familiar sound effects on hand for possible use by their clients during a sound mixing session. Some studios will rent copies of their sound effects to filmmakers who are not their clients.

Finally, filmmakers can provide their own sound effects, as many do, by going to wherever the sounds may actually be heard and recording them on quarter-inch tape. The sounds may then be transferred to 16mm or 35mm magnetic sound film for use in editing them to picture, or for use at a mix.

The author (*right*) and an NBC-TV film crew making a wild recording of the exuberant sounds at a political convention, for later use as sound effects.

Sound equipment of the quality needed for recording voices or music for film is not necessary for the recording of sound effects. If the recordist has adequate access to the sound source, any quarter-inch tape recorder (meant for use by adults), in good working order, usually will record a sound effect quite satisfactorily.

Sound effects are not merely sounds.

As the name indicates, the filmmaker is not so much interested in the sound, *but rather in the* effect *it will have—on the scene, on the action, on the audience of the film.*

And even when a sound effect's function is simply to invest the background of a scene with authenticity, it reflects the controlled reality that can make film production so creative.

11

VOICE OVER FILM

In many cases, narration is in a film what a bear is in a camper's tent: if it is there at all, it is a dominant factor. Although narration and picture should work in perfect tandem, it is often the narration that carries the major burden of communicating what a film is meant to convey.

This is especially true in the case of documentaries. When listening to a typical film documentary with the picture turned off, much if not most of the intended information and comment are successfully communicated by the narration alone. However, when watching it with the sound turned off, few of the scenes, although objectively interesting as pictures, specifically convey what the documentary is supposed to be about.

It is therefore unfortunate that sometimes the writing of narration is accorded much more meticulous attention than the recording of it. Perhaps, because the narration is basically a voice on a piece of quarter-inch tape, some producers consider it less demanding of their time and creative effort than other, more complex, production elements such as synchronous film or optical effects. Or perhaps it is because the recording of the narration often occurs toward the end of the production of a film, and thus must be handled in whatever time, and with whatever attention, is available before the deadline for the film's completion.

In any event, failing to appreciate the importance of narration recording often proves to be that particularly irksome kind of mistake—the one you do not discover has been made until it is too late.

SELECTING A NARRATOR

Performing voice-over-film narration, whether for a ten-second television spot or a two-hour documentary, is a specialized vocation, but one which no longer is associated with any one type of speaking voice.

At one time, a rich, deep voice—the deeper the better—was the traditional hallmark of a professional announcer or narrator, which meant they were exclusively male. This was because the microphones used in earlier broadcasting and recording studios tended to raise the pitch of any voice speaking into them; thus only a deeper voice would sound natural, and only a *very* deep voice would actually sound deep through the microphone.

Today, microphones reproduce the human voice with great fidelity, and while a rich, deep voice is still an asset, many male and female announcer/narrators have become wealthy doing television and radio commercials with voices that are high, scratchy, and which sometimes squeak. This is because such voices are thought to break through to the viewer's or listener's attention in the competitive clutter of the typical station break.

Although a rich, or at least pleasing, speaking voice is still sought for narration on most other types of films, the principal talent of good professional narrators is not the sound of their voices, but in how adept they are at verbally investing words with various tones of meaning.

How a producer goes about finding and selecting a voice-over-film narrator depends upon the locality.

In larger metropolitan areas with frequent or regular production activity, the potential employer of an announcer or narrator should have no problem in finding candidates for the job. Many talent agencies will be found which either partly or totally specialize in representing voice-over and on-camera narrators, of all types and of both sexes. A list of such agencies may be obtained by contacting the local office of the Screen Actors Guild, or the American Federation of Television and Radio Artists.

A visit or telephone call to any of these agencies will usually result in a series of personal interviews with prospective narrators, and the sending of a number of specially-prepared audition tapes containing samples of the narrators' work.

In addition, most professional sound studios will provide the names and telephone numbers of narrators whose work they know, who then may be contacted for interviews or for their audition tapes.

In locales where no such agencies or sound studios exist, some professional announcers may be found at local television and radio stations.

Some producers prefer to first hear tapes, then to meet with those narrators whose tapes interest them. Others prefer to meet with prospective narrators and have them read a page or two of script as part of the interview, perhaps leaving a copy of their audition tape behind as a reference.

It is important to note that a good broadcasting announcer, whether at little WAVN in Stillwater, Minnesota or big KCBS-TV in Los Angeles, is not *necessarily* also a good narrator. Although most of today's successful voice-over-film talent started their careers in radio and television, narration requires special skills—including dramatic ability and voice-control techniques—beyond pleasant tones and a good on-air personality.

Similarly, it is a mistake to assume that any experienced actor, even a good one, necessarily can perform well in the recording booth. An actor certainly might be an excellent narrator, and many of them are. However, a typical actor's training and experience is in using a combination of hands, body movement, voice, and what can only be called projected persona—but an effective narrator must accomplish everything with the voice alone.

No matter who the narrator is, or how he or she is located, a final choice should never be made until after an audition. Interviews, audition tapes, even a brief reading, do not really tell what only an adequate audition can reveal.

First, an audition can indicate whether your prospective narrator can satisfactorily read, not a script, but *your* script. The scripts of the wonderful narrations on an audition tape may not have made the same professional demands that yours will, in part or as a whole.

Even more important, an audition can show whether prospective narrators are *directable.* First, are they personally amenable to repeated interruption for corrections or script changes if necessary without losing their calm, cooperative manner? And even if they are, do they have the necessary skill to *make* the changes satisfactorily?

My idea of the ideal narrator audition is one at which the candidate is heard but not seen. This affords the opportunity to evaluate the voice and the reading exactly as the audience will hear them, totally unaffected by the inevitable human personal response to an individual's appearance, or to some part of it.

No matter where it takes place, only a thorough audition, with the actual material to be recorded, plus a few "changes" prepared as a test, can establish that a particular narrator would be a good choice.

ARRANGING A RECORDING SESSION

A recording session should be well-planned, to minimize the inevitable assault by its traditional enemy—the studio clock. To accomplish this, the session should be arranged to coincide with adequate time in four areas.

Studio Rental There are a number of ways to economize in a film production budget, but the cost of studio rental time is not one of them. Not only do you not want the session to end with that "one more take" left unrecorded, but you want to avoid the atmosphere of tension which results from a narrator's nervous glances at the clock as he or she goes through the script pages that still must be recorded.

Select a time when the studio is available for the full period that you feel, or have been advised, is necessary, with an option to extend the rental time an extra thirty minutes or an hour, if necessary, often referred to as a "bumper."

Studio Facilities You must be sure that you are not only renting a studio, but also all the needed facilities in it or hooked up to it, such as extra tape machines, dubbers, filters, patches to an echo chamber, etc. Nothing is more dismaying than to have a piece of equipment you need suddenly become unavailable in the middle of your session, for use in another studio.

The solution is twofold. First, make certain in advance that you not only have a firm commitment on Studio B from 3:00 p.m. to 6:00 p.m. next Thursday, but also that all the equipment you need will be available in that studio for the entire time period.

Second, to avert any misunderstandings in scheduling, or perhaps a conflict with a sudden need by one of the studio's more regular clients, try to use any special equipment at the start of your studio time, even though it means recording out of script sequence.

Announcer/Narrator's Schedule The studio rental should coincide with the announcer's availability for the full time period, including the optional extension. Busy announcer-narrators sometimes schedule back-to-back recording sessions, in studios that may be in different parts of town. This could mean either that they must arrive a bit late for your session or else must try to leave it early. Either case results in less than ideal conditions for a relaxed, effective recording session.

Studio Engineer's Schedule It is advisable to confirm that your engineer will be assigned to your studio for the entire rental period, as well as for the optional extension if necessary.

A studio's daily rental schedule does not necessarily coincide with their personnel assignment schedule. This means that one engineer might do the first part of your session, and then be scheduled to leave for lunch, or to go home for the day, being relieved by another engineer. Or your engineer may have a particular expertise, not required for your session but needed in another session down the hall, midway in your time period.

The changing of engineers in the middle of a studio session can have an adverse effect on the recording; often the effect, if any, is subtle, but on other occasions it can be significant.

It takes a little time for any recording engineer to prepare the various controls on his or her console, and individual engineers have their own particular ways of setting them up. A new engineer often feels the need to check and perhaps reset the controls upon taking over. This not only impinges on the recording time, but it also causes an interruption in the ongoing pace of the session, a creative momentum that often is not recaptured.

Moreover, the original engineer may be aware of an idiosyncracy of the microphone, or of the recording equipment, or even of the narrator's delivery of certain words—and the replacement may be unaware of, or unable to accommodate, any of them.

And sometimes it is simply a matter of rapport between engineer and producer or narrator. In the demanding atmosphere of a joint creative effort, in the face of inexorably diminishing time, good rapport or the lack of it can make a difference which is reflected on the tape.

IN THE RECORDING STUDIO

There are two methods of recording the narration for a film, and as usual, each has its own relative merits and disadvantages.

The first method is *recording wild,* whereby the narrator's only perspective on the picture during the recording comes from notations in the script describing what will be seen, perhaps with timings to guide the reading.

The alternate method is *recording to picture,* in which the narration is read against the actual film, projected onto a screen the narrator sees as he or she records the script. This is a synchronizing recording, in that the narration is not only recorded but also locked into subsequent synchronization with the picture, by recording a sync signal on the tape.

Before discussing the possible reasons for choosing one over the other, let us examine the two methods of narration recording, as they happen in the studio.

Recording Narration Wild The typical studio designed for recording wild sound is an acoustically protected room, containing a

Recording narration wild in a sound studio. The producer (*right*), with stopwatch in hand, cues the narrator in the recording booth. The recording engineer (*center*) adjusts the sound levels as the film editor watches closely. (Above them are the windows of the projection booth, used when recording to picture.) (Photo by Susan A. Berg at Magno Sound Studios, New York.)

control board console at which the recording engineer sits, controlling the volume and quality of the sound being recorded, which is heard on a large studio loudspeaker.

Nearby is a professional quarter-inch tape recorder, which is used, manually or by remote controls, if the recording is not made directly onto 16mm or 35mm magnetic sound film.

Elsewhere in the room is the recording booth, a small room within a room, containing either a microphone on a table, at which the narrator sits, or a microphone on a boom suspended over a lectern, at which he or she stands during the session. The table or lectern also contains a small desk light to illuminate the script, and often a pair of headphones, so that the narrator can hear voices or other sound from outside the booth while speaking into the microphone, if necessary.

In a well-appointed recording booth, the table will be covered by sound-absorbent felt cloth, to diminish the "bounce" of the sound, and a number of empty acetate page-holders will be available to hold the script pages, eliminating the possibility of paper rattling during the recording.

The booth is, or should be, accoustically isolated from outside sounds by thick walls and door, and windows comprised of at least double, and sometimes triple, layers of glass, between which the trapped air serves as an effective sound barrier.* When the door of the booth is closed, people outside can communicate with the narrator through a "talk-back" microphone at the engineer's console, which is connected to a small speaker inside the booth; the narrator's replies come through the recording microphone.

Except for shorter films, such as ten- to thirty-second commercials and promotional spots, narration is seldom recorded in one long reading of the entire script, but instead is usually recorded in briefer segments, called "takes." This way, the narrator can be coached fully on each part of the script, for example recording and rerecording section "C" until it sounds exactly right, before going on to section "D."

Each time the microphone is turned on to record a take, the engineer records a few seconds of *tone,* a sustained, 1,000 Hz signal tone, after which the narrator prefaces his or her delivery with a *slate,* some form of verbal identification of the take about to be

*For an impression of a studio's facilities, I light a match in front of the recording booth window. Seeing what appear to be two or three flames reflected in the glass is reassuring. Seeing only one flame, usually indicating an ordinary single pane of glass, does not inspire confidence in the studio.

recorded. The most commonly used slates are "Sound" and "Take," as "Sound six" or "Take nine." Quite frequently the studio engineer, instead of the narrator, will deliver each slate (into the control board microphone).

Later, the tone and the slate make it possible to quickly and easily find one particular take on a tape which may contain fifty or even a hundred of them.

For example, wanting to find Sound #16, we play the tape at high speed. The narrator's words are almost unintelligible as they go past the sound head at this speed, but each two seconds of tone is now clearly heard as a high-pitched half-second *beep*. We count sixteen beeps as they go by, then slow the tape to normal speed to hear the narrator's or engineer's voice saying, "Sound sixteen." After a pause, we hear whatever was recorded as that take.

The key to this procedure is the *take sheet,* which is a log made during a recording session that identifies each take on the tape by slate number, notes its time length, and indicates whether or not it is one of the "good" takes scheduled for transfer to 16mm or 35mm magnetic sound film for subsequent use by the film editor.

Take sheets can be improvised on any piece of paper, or can be a form printed especially for the purpose, available at most sound studios. No matter what form it is in, a take sheet is most useful when it is right there with the tape when you need it, and therefore should always be kept in the box with the tape it describes, or fastened to the reel if the tape is not boxed.

It is important not to neglect to note the timings for *every* take, good and bad. To illustrate why, let us say Take #8 was marked as the "good" take for a shot originally planned to run twenty seconds on the screen. But later, in editing the film, the shot must be shortened to seventeen seconds. Take #8, as good as it sounds, no longer is usable because it is too long. We look at the take sheet to see the timings of some of the other takes containing the same words, and find that Take #6, which was rejected because it seemed a bit rushed, took exactly fifteen seconds.

Not having it on magnetic sound film in the editing room because it was not marked for transfer from the quarter-inch tape, we get the tape and listen to Take #6. It is almost as good a delivery as Take #8, and it is the right length. The quarter-inch tape is sent out to have Sound #6 transferred to magnetic sound film, and work goes on without unnecessary delay, such as going through the entire tape with a stopwatch, checking various takes to find a possible replacement.

Take Sheet

Talent	Studio	Recording Day and Date	Time	
			From	To

Take No.	Time	Print	NG	Identification	

Tape Identification	
Original	Protection

A take sheet.

A take sheet can be even more valuable when it includes terse notations about the delivery of some of the takes.

For example, during editing of a film we find that the subject of a certain scene is no longer to be presented as a prime example of impressive "bigness" (which now will be conveyed in some other scene). But in the track containing the take selected for use over that scene we hear the word "big" being emphasized by the narrator, as was requested. Once again we look at the take sheet, and see the notation *'big' not stressed as hard* next to a take that was not considered for use, but now may be just what we want. Seeing those few words will now save us considerably more time than the moments it took to write them.

Recording Narration to Picture A recording studio equipped to accommodate a session in which the narration is read to picture is very similar to one in which narrations are recorded wild, and may in fact often be used for both kinds of recordings. There are, however, some features that differentiate it from a studio designed only for wild recording.

First, near the far wall is a projection screen. Near the screen, an illuminated digital footage counter is clearly visible, to indicate exactly which frame of the film is on the screen at any time.

Overlooking the studio, high on the wall behind the control console, is the window of a projection booth, an adjoining room containing a 16mm and/or 35mm projector; an assortment of lenses for various needs, such as adjusting the projected picture for wide screen viewing in the studio; a small table on which electric or hand-cranked reel rewinds are attached; and a few items of basic film splicing equipment, for emergency repairs on any tears in the film that may occur during a session.

Nearby there may be a clients' editing room which is more extensively equipped, into which a film editor can hurry to correct some error in the picture or tracks which was noticed during the session, or possibly to make some change important enough to warrant a delay in the studio proceedings.

Near the microphone inside the recording booth is a small red or white *cue light,* which may be used to signal the narrator when to speak in each scene during the running of the film.

Before the picture is projected, the narrator does a run-through of the script, at which time the producer may coach him or her on the delivery of certain lines, which will not be as easy to do once the simultaneous voice recording and picture projection begin.

Directing a narration recorded to picture is somewhat more demanding than directing a wild recording session, where the producer's primary concern is to elicit the right reading of the lines within the desired timings. When recording to picture, however, there are these same requirements plus one other: the various segments must also start and end at exactly the right time in relation to the picture on the screen.

For example, Scene #11 shows an airliner coming in for a

landing, then coming to a sharp halt at its assigned place on the runway. The narration over the scene is: "Flying these big birds is an important job . . . and a tough one."

The line runs five seconds. The scene runs fifteen seconds. The last four words, " . . . and a tough one," are supposed to coincide with the plane's sudden halt on the runway, and the producer must be sure that the narrator both begins and ends the entire line so that it all hits just right in the scene.

When recording wild, a good narrator usually can determine how most lines should sound without undue coaching, but he or she can only guess at where any line should start and end in relation to the picture. Thus, a narrator's need for guidance during a session is greatly increased when recording to picture.

The producer, having personally rehearsed the narration against the film at a Moviola, has selected the ideal "hitting" points of various lines, and can either write these cues on the script, requiring the narrator to watch for specific action on the screen, or also use the cue light to signal when the narrator should start speaking into the microphone each time.

All in all, recording to picture can be a challenging experience for a narrator, who must work with one eye on the screen and one eye on the script—plus, somehow, another eye on the control room for specific signals or general reaction.

In addition, at a wild recording session, when a narrator gets a signal to begin, he or she usually takes an adequate breath, mentally prepares how the line should sound, and then calmly starts to speak. When recording to picture, however, the cue light is somewhat like an urgent voice suddenly ordering, "Start talking *now!*"

At a smaller or less fully equipped studio, the atmosphere when recording to picture can be charged with pressure—the result of everyone fervently hoping each time the film starts to roll that this pass will be *the* one, in which everything works as it should from beginning to end.

If not, if during the running of the film nineteen out of the twenty narration segments are perfect but the twentieth is not, the whole thing has to be aborted, the film brought back to the head—usually by taking the reel off the projector, putting it on manual rewinds to be wound back to the start, then threading it up on the projector once more—and tried again from the beginning.

This is because, using the quarter-inch tape equipment familiar for so many years in professional studios, any synchronous recording of picture and sound must be accomplished in one uninterrupted take.

There are a number of reasons why the film projector and tape machine cannot be stopped in the middle of such a recording, backed up to rerecord where a line did not hit just right, then made to go forward again.

For one, each stopping or starting of the recorder would produce a heavy *click* on the tape, impossible to satisfactorily remove. It could be physically cut out, *if* in the clear, but that could throw the recording on the tape that much out of true sync with the picture.

Then, although the tape has a sync signal on it for later alignment with the picture, during the recording the tape and the film are completely independent of each other, mechanically and electronically. Thus if they are stopped in the middle of a joint run, each backed up to a desired point, and then started forward again, it would only be the most miraculous chance if they again were in exactly the same relationship as before the interruption.

However, the development of the *back-up interlock system* now makes it possible to do just that: interrupt a synchronous recording by stopping the picture and all sources of sound (whether from a "live" narrator or any kind of prerecorded tracks), back them up to erase and redo a bad take—all the while maintaining their exact relative positions—and then resume recording.

The key to the system is that the recording is made, not on quarter-inch tape, which does not have sprocket holes, but on 16mm or 35mm magnetic sound film, which do.

The sprocket holes on the recorded track, like those on all the other tracks used in the session, have exactly the same uniform regularity as the sprocket holes on the film in the projector. Thus the system can relate to a specific point on any sound track to a specific frame of the picture, and, by exercising sophisticated electro-mechanical control of them, move them in either direction without losing synchronization.

In addition, each time the engineer pushes the button to start or stop recording, the signal is electronically cross-faded in or out, thus avoiding any *click*.

Unfortunately, the back-up interlock system is not available at every sound studio, especially smaller ones.

When the recording to picture is completed, the synchronized track (after transfer to 16mm or 35mm magnetic sound film if recorded on quarter-inch tape) is turned over to the film editor, who merely has to mark the point where a *bleep* signals the start of synchronous sound, align that mark with the start mark on the film, and the track automatically is in perfect sync with the picture.

To more clearly compare the two methods for recording narration, the narration was the only sound synchronized to the film in our discussion of recording to picture. However, while this does happen, it is not typical. More often, such a recording session is called a *live mix,* because *all* the sound elements in a film are brought to the studio to simultaneously join the live narration in being recorded to picture.

Thus, a live mix is often selected not only as an alternative to a wild recording session, but as a combination of both that recording *and* the sound mix that normally would later follow. That, in fact, is its major advantage: after one session in the sound studio, the producer leaves with a final sound mix of all the elements.

Since it combines two production steps in one, a live mix saves money, which is probably its primary attraction to many of the producers who use it. What often makes it attractive even to producers with unlimited budgets is that a live mix also saves time.

However, like most convenient two-in-one combinations, a live mix can be something of a compromise in both areas.

First, the quality of the narration may be less than the optimum possible. A narrator, no matter how talented and experienced, cannot give a script the concentration which is possible when recording wild. The narrator's reading may be good—but it probably would be even better without the need to continually rotate his or her attention between the script, the screen, the control room and the clock.

Then, the quality of the total sound mix is a factor to consider. As we shall see in the next chapter, the engineer at the average mix is handling a six-ring circus of sound and picture—but at least he or she can control what is happening in each ring. At a live mix, however, there is an element the engineer *cannot* control with equal precision—the narration. When it comes in, where it comes in, how it comes in, even the volume at which it comes in, are all variables each time the mix is attempted.

Once again, in choosing between the two methods of recording narration, the producer must decide whether the savings in time and money are worth the possible trade-offs in potential quality.

Directing the Narrator The narration for many local television commercials is directed by the producer, who usually works for the product's advertising agency (and frequently *is* the advertising agency).

When commercials for major accounts, prepared by large advertising agencies, are recorded, the direction could come from any one of a number of possibilities: a professional director who is a member of the Directors Guild of America, the agency producer, the account's art director, the copywriter—or someone else, in the restlessly churning area of creative responsibility found at so many large advertising agencies.

In the case of a typical nontheatrical film, while sometimes a director is hired for the recording session, quite often the person on the other side of the studio glass, directing and coaching the narrator, is the film's producer.

It is ironic that so many producers of nontheatrical films achieve maximum effectiveness from every element of film production except the one which is often the most important of all—the narration.

I think this is because some producers, who may be skillful in their use of other materials or procedures, apparently approach the recording of the narration with an entirely different attitude. After all, most other aspects of film production generally entail dealing with *things,* such as film footage, tracks, and assorted equipment. But the narrator sitting there before the microphone is a *person,* often a man or woman the producer knows quite well. And so, as the recording session proceeds, the producer naturally relates to the narrator as a fellow human being, rather than as some "tool" in the production process.

And that can be a mistake. For as they engage in a few pleasant minutes of friendly talk in the studio before and after the session, narrators of course *are* people. But when the red light is on, signalling that the microphone is live and the recording machines are turning, the narrator is not good old Vic or Norman or Joyce or Wally, but a controllable production element, one that can affect the impact of every part of the film.

In our everyday dealings with people, when we ask someone to do something, and they do it not *precisely* as we envisioned they might, we generally accept it, for to do otherwise might rightfully be considered rigid or dictatorial. However, it is not always wise to carry this ordinarily desirable attitude into a recording session, where it can result in little compromises you subsequently regret. Many a line, read almost the way the director wants, later confirms the adage, "Almost doesn't count," when during screenings it does not work as well as it could with the picture.

Experience will show that most professional narrators and announcers welcome all the meaningful direction they can get. Nothing dismays them more than a director who demonstrates uncertainty about what is wanted—usually by indicating quite clearly that the reading is not right, without just as clearly conveying why it is wrong.

Too many directors enter the recording studio without a specific idea of what they want in every part of the script reading, feeling that as the session proceeds they will know what they like when they hear it. This kind of "recording roulette" may produce the right reading within the first few takes, *if* a perceptive narrator deduces what might sound right. But it is more likely that it will only happen after ten or fifteen takes of each segment—if it happens at all.

Instead, the director should go over the script before the recording session and analyze each line, deciding in advance how it should be read. Then, in the studio, he or she will mentally "hear" the right reading for each take before it is recorded, and thus be able to convey to the narrator exactly what is wanted.

Quite often, the question at a recording session is not so much what the director wants, but rather how to communicate this to the narrator.

Before the narrator enters the recording booth, most directors discuss the overall "feel" the narration should have.* But for the specific changes which inevitably will be wanted during the session, *good directors communicate to the narrator, not the word sounds they want to hear, but a clear sense of the effect they want the words to achieve.*

For example, in discussing the reading of the word *powerful,* instead of telling the narrator, "Emphasize 'powerful' a bit more," they might say, "Make it more important."

To merely tell the narrator to emphasize a word indicates only that you want it read differently—but not *how* it should be read differently. As with most adjectives, a word like "powerful" can be emphasized in various ways, each implying an entirely different context—"strong," "big," "important," "influential," etc.

Therefore, when a director simply asks for it to be "emphasized" or "hit harder" or "punched up," which all convey the same generality, the narrator, who usually is aware of the various possible connotations, will try each one in turn, until he or she happens on the one that sounds right to the director. If this chances to fall on the third try, the director thinks, "It took this narrator three takes to get it right." But the narrator thinks, "If he had told me *that* was what he wanted, I would have given it to him on the first take."

*I find that playing a sample of the music selected for the film helps in conveying to the narrator the general approach I want the reading to take.

A good director will use line readings only as a last resort. Simply stated, a line reading is a director telling a narrator or an actor, "Say it like this . . ." and then speaking the line for them to copy. The method is clear, direct, and avoids any possibility of misunderstanding. At the same time, asking that he or she merely mimic what you say ignores the significant creative contribution that any good narrator has to offer. More times than I can remember, a narrator has pleasantly surprised me with a delivery that achieved the requested effect in a different and much better way than I had envisioned.

Finally, there must be a quality, maintained scene by scene in the entire narration, that consistently reflects the approach, the overall tone, that you envisioned coming from the screen. For what you are dealing with, as you listen on this side of the glass, is not the voice of some narrator. It is the voice of your film.

12 THE MIXING OF SOUND

Although we talk about a completed film's *track*, it is really more like a sonic Grand Central Station, in which many tracks of sound have converged from various sources, followed by the skillful blend of them all into one continuous flow of picture-and-sound—the final mix.

IN THE MIXING STUDIO

The typical professional studio equipped to mix film sound has been described earlier. However, while the producer's view of the process is confined to what takes place in the studio, the mix actually happens simultaneously in two places—the studio and the *dubbing room.*

This important room contains the film sound reproducing machines, more popularly called *dubbers,* which record and play back the 16mm or 35mm tracks used during a mix. One machine, the recording dubber, contains blank 16mm or 35mm magnetic sound film, onto which the mix will be recorded.

Before the start of the session, the tracks containing a film's various sound elements are brought to the dubbing room, where

The dubbing room of a large and busy sound recording complex, containing eighty dubbers to accommodate the recording and mixing needs of five studios. (Photo by Susan A. Berg at Magno Sound Studios, New York.)

each track is put on a separate machine. The output of each machine is then routed to one of the inputs on the control board in the studio, from where it will be remotely controlled during the mix.

At the control console in the studio sits the mixer,* whose actual professional title is "re-recording mixer," since the sound elements about to be mixed have all been recorded previously. The sound coming from any of the dubbers into an input on the control panel arrives at maximum volume, and its sound level is then regulated by the control most frequently used during a mix, usually called a "pot" (a shortening of its technical name, *potentiometer*).

*In New York, film sound mixes (including complicated ones) are usually handled by one mixer. In California, however, it is not unusual to have three mixers in attendance at a session, each handling either voices, music, or sound effects.

There are, in fact, a number of controls at each input. On a well-equipped studio control board, adjoining each pot will be:

1. A multi-switched equalizer, for boosting or removing high, medium, or low frequencies, to better equalize, or balance, the relative volumes of adjacent sounds.
2. A switch to add reverberation to the sound.
3. A switch to provide echo.
4. Special sound filters to eliminate unwanted frequencies.
5. An on-off switch, which can completely close the input to any sound coming from the dubber to which it is patched.

In addition to this series of identical controls, one group for each input, the panel will contain VU meters to monitor sound levels, and three or four sound compressors.

A typical control board at a busy studio will have eighteen inputs, although twenty-four is not unusual.

However, there is little point to having a board with a lot of inputs if it is patched into a dubbing room which only contains a few dubbers. One sound company in New York, typical of a large facility in an active film production area, has eighty machines in the dubbing

The control console at a professional sound studio, used for recording or mixing motion picture sound. (Photo by Susan A. Berg at Magno Sound Studios, New York.)

room, for its five studios. Some studio complexes in the Los Angeles area have even more dubbers, but most sound companies have considerably fewer, since they generally have only one to three studios.

Sitting at, or near, the console are the producer and the film editor, waiting to watch the screen for the first rehearsal.

The tracks are being threaded onto the dubbers, and the mixer, using an intercom built into the control panel, talks with the dubbing room, to ask which tracks are on which machines, noting this information on a piece of paper, or marking it with crayon on the smooth countertop in front of the appropriate control knobs.

The various tracks for a mix are usually labelled by letters, such as Music "B" or Effects "A," rather than by numbers. This is because the knobs of the pots on a studio control board often have factory-printed numbers on them, and while dealing with "Narration B on Pot 4" presents no problem, "Narration 2 on Pot 4" could invite confusion during the fast-moving activity of a mix.

Just as important as knowing where the various tracks are channeled into the control board is knowing where each one should come in and go out in each scene of the film. This is indicated on the *mixing cue sheet* prepared by the film editor and used as an essential reference by the sound engineer throughout the mix.

The cue sheet is a combination timetable/road map of all the film's tracks, showing in parallel columns the points at which each sound starts, ends, or is crossed over into another sound—each point marked by an indication of how many feet it is from the film's start mark, which is zero on the footage counter.

A good cue sheet does not contain descriptions of the accompanying picture, which can be seen on the screen, nor notations about volume levels, which may be discussed verbally. Thus, the footage count numbers indicating where the tracks go in and out, the last few words on each voice track, and terse descriptions of sound effects when more than one are used at the same time, all will clearly meet the eye of the mixer in the dimly lit room as he or she glances down at the cue sheet during a mix.

For example, for a thirty-minute film, a cue sheet might indicate that:

> *MUSIC "A"* comes in at 270, and is joined at 360 by *EFFECTS "C"*.
> At 630, *EFFECTS "D"* is added.
> At 810, the effects tracks both go out, and *MUSIC "A"* is cross-faded into *MUSIC "B"*, etc.

In the film during the mix, this translates into:

> *HEROIC MUSIC THEME* comes in at 270 [scene of the soldiers preparing for combat], and is joined at 360 [battle scene] by *COMBAT SOUNDS.*
>
> At 630, *CLANKING OF TANKS* is added.
>
> At 810, the effects tracks both go out, and *HEROIC MUSIC THEME* is cross-faded into *ROMANTIC MUSIC THEME* [for the love scene], etc.

Thus, during a mix, the engineer is looking at the cue sheet, the meters, the controls, and the illuminated footage counter below the screen much more often than at the screen itself.

SOUND LOOPS

The last column of the cue sheet may indicate that one of the tracks, usually a sound effect, is to be handled differently than the other tracks.

There are two kinds of sound effects. One is a specific, individual sound, such as a gunshot or a cry. Since its exact location in relation to picture has been established, the film editor will align it with the appropriate shot, the gun being fired or the person crying out. It will then be brought to the mix fixed in its place on the effects track, along with other such effects on the track.

The other kind of effect involves a more continuous sound, such as mob shouting or rolling thunder, which may be used, not only in one scene, but intermittently in various scenes. Ideally it should be set in against specific picture at each required place in the film. Instead, however, such a sound effect is often made into a *loop.* This means it is recorded on a short length of track, after which the beginning and end of the track are spliced together, thus forming an endless loop which will run continuously on a playback machine.

Room tone and presence, which are usually recorded in brief amounts at a filming site, are very often used on loops.

A sound loop may be used in either of two ways at a mix:

First, the loop may be kept wild. While the appropriate scene is undergoing the usual trial mixes and re-mixes, the other tracks go backwards and forward in sync with the picture each time. But the loop is continuously running forward, and the mixer simply opens a pot each time that sound is wanted, lets it play as long as necessary, then closes the pot again.

This presents no problem if the sound on the loop is fairly

PROD. NO. S 340

PRODUCER GOODSHOT PRODS

TITLE CAR SAFETY

NAR	A DIA	B DIA	A MUSIC	B MUSIC	A. FX.	B. FX.
SYNC BEEP 9	9	9	9	9	9	9
			12			
22^{10} – 30^{4} ROAD						
			42^{6} →	→	42^{6} F1 TRAFFIC	42^{6} F1 FOOT STEPS
	48^{2} – 50^{6} ME	50^{6} – 58^{9} LONG				
	58^{9} – 61^{4} MONDAY	61^{4} – 64 GIRL				61^{11}
	64 – 66^{8} HELP			67	66^{10}	66^{8} CRASH
					68 – 70 THUMP	
73^{6} – 84 UNEVEN			73			73^{8}

A typical cue sheet for a sound mix.

uniform, such as the regular blowing of the wind. But let us say, for example, that it is the sound of surf crashing against rocks on the shore. This is a more or less continuous sound, but not all of the crashes heard in endlessly repeating series are *exactly* the same. Perhaps two of them have a somewhat heavier, more dramatic impact, which works well against some specific action on the screen. If the loop is used wild, one of these "good" crashes may, or may not, hit with that action each time.

In such a case, the loop will be *locked on the line.* This means that once the mixer has aligned the desired part of the loop with the appropriate action, by adjusting picture and sound until they "hit" together, the loop remains in sync, along with the other tracks, as the scene is mixed and remixed.

Whether used as loops or not, some sound effects are virtually created anew at a mixing session. Through the versatility of the sound-processing equipment, and the skill of many of the engineers who use it, a sound effect may be so ingeniously revised during a mix as to be unrecognizable as the sound it originally was, which failed to work as anticipated.

THE PRE-MIX

The average nontheatrical film may have six or seven tracks. Other films, such as documentaries or certain types of movies, often have many more. However, the producer of any kind of film may arrive at a sound studio with more tracks than there are dubbers available on which to play them back during the mix. This may be either because the dubbing room simply does not contain enough machines, or perhaps it does but most of them are being used for mixes in the other studios.

In any event, the solution is a *pre-mix* of some of the tracks. For example, two or three of the sound tracks will be selected to be run with the picture for a separate mix, which is recorded. Then this mixed track is used along with the other, waiting, tracks in a second mix—which produces a final mixed track of all the film's sound elements.

If a pre-mix is necessary, it is best to pre-mix voice tracks. Voices are usually the most significant sounds in any film, and it is important that they be loud enough to be distinctly heard and always kept in the clear in relation to other sounds. Therefore, if a film or scene to be pre-mixed contains narration, dialogue, or other synchronized speech, these tracks would be balanced for proper volume and equalization, then mixed and recorded, after which music and sound effects would be added in a subsequent mix.

Music and sound effects are not desirable choices for pre-mixing. This is because judgments about whether music or effects sound "right" in a film are largely based on their relationship to other sounds, not on how they sound alone, as in the case of voices.

REHEARSAL AND FINAL MIX

The projectionist comes on the intercom to report that the projector has been threaded up and the film is ready to roll.

Quite often this is a work print. However, many producers will have a black-and-white duplicate print made from the work print, especially for use at the mix. This print is quickly struck off, with no real concern for tonal contrast in the scenes, and being a duplicate, it shows all the marks made on the work print by the editor's marking pencil. None of which matters. What does matter is that, being a newly made print, it is one continuous length of splice-free film, and therefore better able to be projected, and moved back and forth on the machine, without possibly slipping or threatening to tear, as a work print might.

The lights go down in the studio for the first rehearsal.

A master remote control switch on the console simultaneously starts the projector and all the dubbers. Because it is an electro-mechanical *interlock* system, all the playback machines will start, come up to speed, and maintain the speed for constant synchronization with each other and with the film projector—all in perfect unison.

The mixer keeps all the pots open wide, noting the levels of various tracks as they come in. The purpose of the rehearsal is to familiarize the mixer with what the picture looks like, generally where the different tracks come in, and most important, the relationship between picture and sound in the various scenes.

In addition, during the rehearsal the mixer constantly checks the footage counter, comparing what is happening on the screen with what appears on the cue sheet.

As a result of each rehearsal, some adjustments are usually made. Perhaps music "A," marked to fade in at 315 feet, should really fade in a bit earlier, at 309, to slightly lead into some bit of action instead of coming in exactly when the action does. Accordingly, the mixer moves the track containing music "A" back six feet for the mixing of that scene. Without the interlock system, mixers simply ask the dubbing room, through the intercom, to wind the track back by hand.

As the session proceeds, the producer and the film editor observe the ongoing mix closely. They have played all the sound elements against the film many times in the cutting room, in interlock. But on the Moviola or editing table, the marriage of picture and track is only an approximation of how the multiple sounds will really work, individually and with each other. Now, for the first time, they hear each sound with optimal adjustment of its volume, balance, and equalization with other sounds, and observe with particular interest how certain music or sound effects interact with the specific action to which they are keyed.

A well-equipped studio for mixing film sound will have a smaller speaker, with a more limited range, in addition to the big studio speaker. Each time a completed mix is played back for approval, on the studio speaker that has been used throughout the session, experienced producers will ask to hear the mix played on the smaller speaker as well, for a more realistic example of how it would sound as the track printed on a film.

THE SOUND CAMERA

When the mixer uses the intercom to the projection booth and dubbing room to announce, "That's a wrap," the studio may have one more important service to perform.

Each release print of the film that has just been mixed will emerge from the lab with an optical sound track printed along one side. Seen under a strong glass, a sound track appears as a series of modulation lines resembling the jagged peaks on a graph. It is, in fact, a picture of sound, and to print it on the film requires an *optical sound negative.*

This special negative is produced on an *optical sound track recorder,* found at many professional film labs and at larger sound studios, which can translate sound into photo-image (and therefore was first also known by the more interestingly descriptive name, "sound camera").

At a sound studio, it is used to transfer a completed recording or mix from magnetic track to a 16mm or 35mm optical sound negative, which is sent to the lab for their use (along with the picture negative they already have) in making the composite prints of a film.

The sound mix has a special significance, for it is usually the culmination of a film's creative production.

The next step is the lab, and what all the preceding steps have led to—the release prints.

13 IN THE LAB

To film producers, the release prints awaited from the commercial motion picture laboratory are somewhat like the contents of an unopened gift package: after much anticipation, they want it—yet they're half afraid to look for fear of being disappointed.

Before that moment of truth, however, the typical filmmaker has many dealings with a lab during a film's production, starting with the processing and printing of footage shot during filming sessions.

CAMERA ORIGINAL

The film coming out of the camera for processing by a lab is properly called *camera original;* calling it "negative," as many do, only invites possible confusion at the one place where precise understanding is especially wanted. For example, to someone at a lab, 16mm reversal that has been exposed in the camera is not really negative; moreover, references to "negative" could, at a lab, mean camera original, internegative, duplicate negative, optical sound negative, or printing negative. "Camera original," however, has one unmistakable meaning.

An active concern for the protection of negative material is traditional in film production, and the closer a negative is to original material, the greater the care it receives. Since camera original is the most original of all, an experienced filmmaker keeps it in the safest possible place, which is usually the storage vault of the lab. There, it is secure against misplacement in the cutting room or production office, and is stored under the proper climatic conditions for film material. In addition, it is then readily available to lab personnel when needed. Commercial motion picture labs often charge no fee for the storage of clients' film material during production.

DAILIES

When camera original is sent to the lab for processing, each roll is developed into a negative, but not everything on each roll will be printed. The camera original is usually accompanied by a *camera report,* the film equivalent of the take sheet used at sound recording sessions, identifying which takes of each scene, as indicated by the slates, are to be printed.

These prints of the "good" takes selected from whatever was filmed during a shooting session are called *dailies.* Since they are sometimes put into the lab for quick developing and printing, often overnight, with the emphasis on speed in providing the prints rather than the niceties of correct exposure, they are also called *rushes.*

Since each take that is printed costs money, theoretically it is prudent to select only the "good" takes, ones which you know should definitely be printed for possible use. In this case, however, economic wisdom could be creative error, for sometimes what looks perfect in the camera does not quite work out on the cutting table. Often a similar shot, not judged to be as good at the time, would be better with a narration line, or would cut better from the previous shot; but it is not readily available, for it was never printed.

While some filmmakers instruct the lab to print all takes except those known to be technically marred, I, like many others, follow a middle ground of printing the good takes plus a liberal sampling of second choices as well.

Because black-and-white is substantially less expensive to print than color, some producers routinely order black-and-white dailies. Since this is the source material for the work print, their films are therefore shot in color but edited in black-and-white.

However, unless there are budgetary restraints, black-and-white prints from color camera original have at least two disadvantages. A black-and-white print made from a color negative tends to be grainier than a color print would be, making evaluation of the dailies uncertain to some degree. In addition, during editing it is obviously impossible to make creative judgments about relative color values of adjacent shots and scenes.

TIMING AND COLOR CORRECTION

Two primary evaluations we make in looking at our photos picked up from the corner drugstore concern their *density*, relating to how dark or light each picture appears, and whether we aprove of the color in each one. The same considerations apply to motion picture film—except these judgments apply not to individual frames of picture, but to the relative density and color relationship between groups of pictures, which form scenes.

The control of the density of each scene and of the film as a whole is known as *timing*. The timer, a key member of the lab staff, governs how light or dark each scene will be by controlling the printing light to which the film material is exposed, compensating for the varying density of the original material. His or her decisions are subjective, based on experience and a judgment of what degree of light or dark a particular scene requires. Similar judgments are made about the color values in each scene.

At the larger labs, instructions are then punched into a tape for automatic control of scene-to-scene timing and color adjustment during the printing process.

While timing and color correction are not precisely the same thing, they are closely interrelated, for a change in density of a scene affects the color values to some degree, and specific alteration of a scene's color can affect how light or dark it appears.

Producers who are particularly concerned about timing or color correction often make arrangements to be at the side of the timer during the initial timing of their film, approving or requesting changes in what the timer decides for each scene.

In ordering the dailies, from which the work print is made, a producer may either ask the lab to provide a print that is fully timed and color-corrected, or one that is not, accepting instead a *one-light print.* In making a one-light print, the entire roll of film is printed with the same printing light (which may be the one used as an average light), with no attempt made to adjust the density of each scene.

Since it is less expensive than a timed print, and is more quickly produced, a one-light print is used by a great many filmmakers for work print material, with timing and color correction held off until the making of the release prints.

Fully timed prints for all dailies are sometimes ordered by producers who are concerned about the ability of a client or a corporate superior to properly evaluate a work print—no matter how carefully the producer explains that what is seen now is not the quality to be expected in the completed film.

THE ANSWER PRINT

The procedure surrounding the release printing, like the coda of a symphony, is the climax toward which all the preceding creative effort has led, and it is marked by the arrival from the lab of an *answer print*—the first sample of how the completed film will look and sound.

It is called an answer print because the lab, which presumably considers it to be acceptable in timing, color, and overall quality, is asking the producer, "Should we proceed to print the full quantity based on this print as a model?" Often, the answer is no, until at least three such prints are submitted and corrected.

In screening an answer print, the producer carefully examines many aspects of the film, but six areas are of most interest.

Timing Not only is the film checked for over- or under-lighting of individual scenes, but the lighting of each scene is noted in relationship to adjacent scenes.

Color The producer checks for accuracy of color tones, using either a universal criterion, such as the green of the grass, or something in the film whose color is familiar to him or her, but perhaps not to the lab personnel. In addition, overall color qualities are noted, such as scenes that have a red or orange cast, making them too "hot," or a bluish tone, which means they are too "cool."

Optical Effects Unless a special optical check print has been made by the optical house, the answer print offers the first opportunity to see all the opticals printed on film. The producer not only looks for mistakes in the optical effects, but also notes whether they generally work as anticipated.

Negative Matching Sometimes there may be an obvious error in matching the negative to the work print, usually caused by misreading an edge number. The subsequent wrong placement of a shot within a scene can result in some bizarre on-screen action. Usually, however, it is a more subtle error, which an audience might not even recognize as a mistake.

Sound Track Besides usually providing the first view of the visual elements in their final form, the composite answer print also provides the first opportunity to really hear the sound track as it will be heard every time the film is projected.

The producer listens for overall quality, especially noting whether the track, as printed on the film by the laboratory, has lost any more of its high and low ranges than should be expected.

Just as important, the answer print is closely checked for synchronization between sound and picture in 'lip sync,' sound effects, and music.

Scratches Scratches on a film are never desirable, but sometimes they may be tolerated if made by the camera while shooting something considered indispensable, scratched or not.

However, when unexpected scratches are seen while screening an answer print, the projector is usually stopped immediately to investigate a crucial question: is the scratch *on* the film, or *in* the film?

If physically *on* the film, there may be a sigh of relief, because it means the scratch is only on that particular print, perhaps made only moments ago. However, if the scratch is seen in the picture, but is *not* physically on the film, it is a more serious matter, for that means the scratch is probably on the negative.

In that case, the next important question is: what color is the scratch? A white line (in a color film) probably means the scratch is on the base side, or back, of the negative, and can possibly be polished away by a special process available at many labs.

However, a dark or colored line in the answer print usually means that the scratch is on the emulsion, or front, of the negative, for which the remedy is a much chancier matter. Depending on how wide and deep the scratch is, its effect may be minimized by use of a *liquid gate.*

In liquid gate printing (also called *wet gate* printing), before the scratched black-and-white or color negative is exposed, it is coated with a liquid that has a similar *refractive index,* which refers to how a medium's density affects the angle at which light passes through it. The scratch being filled in by a liquid with similar light-refracting properties reduces the *scatter,* or irregularity of the light going through, at that point.

The more shallow a scratch, and the more inconspicuous its

position in the picture, the more invisible this process can make it. However, a more formidable gouge on the emulsion side of a negative may mean that the shot cannot be used in the scene, and an alternate shot may have to be selected from the original material and then the printing process repeated to provide another answer print.

RELEASE PRINTING

Since the negative of a completed film is a valuable asset, representing many hours of creative and technical effort, steps are often taken to keep it from the handling and possible damage of the printing process.

In this protective procedure, the original negative of the produced film is used to make a *master positive,* a special, higher-density positive, designed specifically to be the source of subsequent negatives used in printing.

In color film production, the master positive is called *inter-positive* and has a characteristic orange hue. In black-and-white film production, the master positive is called *fine grain* and has a pale purple color.

The original negative is then safely stored, and from the master positive comes the negative or negatives used in making the release prints.

If, for some reason, a producer should decide to have release prints made directly from the original negative, a master positive might still be made and then stored away, to be used in the event some mishap befalls the original negative during printing.

Similar protective procedures may be used when working with reversal film by using internegatives instead of the original reversal for the printing process.

Finally, your last step in the stimulating, time-consuming, rewarding, demanding, but always fascinating process is reached, and what started as concept becomes reality.

Release prints arrive, ready for projection and posterity.

A film has been produced.

THE END

INDEX